of

PRAYER

FOR COUPLES

Building relational intimacy
and spiritual oneness
through prayer.

DENNIS AND BILLIE HENDERSON

FOREWORD BY DENNY HENDERSON

STRATEGIC RENEWAL

STRATEGIC RENEWAL

© 2022 by Dennis and Billie Henderson

Published by Strategic Renewal

www.strategicrenewal.com

Printed in the United States of America

ISBN 9780981609089

Contents

DEDICATION

*To our four children, Stephanie, Shannon, Sharon,
and Denny, who endured growing up in a pastor's home
and for whom we continue to pray daily
as they follow Jesus.*

*To Troy and Janel Keaton who have impacted our lives
as they live to glorify Jesus. Like Billie and me,
they live life in circumstances we never imagined.
As they pray, we pray that God will be honored in our lives.
They are our encouragement from 1,500 miles away.
Thank you, Troy and Janel. You are our models of endurance
and faithfulness. Let's finish well. Acts 20:24*

Foreword

Charles Spurgeon, the prince of preachers, once said regarding perseverance in ministry:

"I do not think that anything but death would get me to go away from this spot. I hardly agree with ministers when they get beaten, showing the white feather, and resigning their charge. I feel that I am the captain of a vessel; and if there should be a Jonah in the ship, I shall, as gently and in as Christian a spirit as possible, pitch him out; I shall not think, because Jonah is there, that therefore I ought to leave, but I will stand by the ship in ill weather as well as in sunshine."

I love Spurgeon's pastoral resolve. This type of determination is required to persevere in pastoral ministry. It is rare in today's world that we find such examples of "finishing the race" set before us in ministry.

For the last 47 years, I have been blessed by the Lord to have a father who put his life before me as a model of what it means to have great resolve in ministry. Each pastor experiences the great heights of victories and the great depths of struggle, challenges, and trials. I have often asked, "How has my father served the Lord with steadfastness for well over 50 years?" Now that I am well into my forties, with 26 years of ministry under my belt, I am finally seeing with clarity the secret of running the race with the joy that my father has demonstrated for me—the secret: a Proverbs 31 wife and the sustaining power of prayer.

Behind every godly man and pastor is a strong, courageous wife and stands on her own two feet. Even more significant is a wife that spends more time on her knees in prayer with the Lord than relying upon the strength of her feet. For over 55 years, my mother has been the powerful force of our family. She could be described as quiet and meek to the casual observer, but she is bold and fearless in the closet of prayer. It has been the prayers of a wife that have sustained my father's strength. It has been the steadfastness of my mother, spending time with her heavenly father daily, pouring out her heart in prayer that has rescued me from many troubles. Solomon wrote in Proverbs 31:10, "A wife of noble character who can find?" Well, my father found her, and she has been instrumental to their successful life of ministry.

The second secret to being steadfast to God's calling is prayer. EM Bounds once wrote, "Prayer puts God's work in His hands and keeps it there. It looks to Him constantly and depends on Him implicitly to further His cause." We are desperate people, which includes desperate pastors and leaders. We can become discouraged, weary, and burdened with the great work that God has called us to do. But didn't Jesus say, "My yoke is easy, and my burden is light?" On Monday mornings, it doesn't feel so easy or so light. But the leader who endures, the man or woman who finishes the race, is the one that places the Lord's work back in his hands through persistent, passionate, and urgent prayer. Prayer is the power and sustenance for anyone who desires to walk faithfully for the Lord.

What a gift I have been given by the Lord to have a father and a mother who not only had a commitment to their calling but a commitment to one another in marriage. What began as a budding love at 18 years old, fresh out of high school, has now become a strong oak that has not been blown over by the strong winds of life and ministry. Prayer has been the forceful power of their ministry and marriage.

As you read this book, you can rest assured that these words are not coming from scholars who have been stuffed away in the halls of academia. Instead, the words of encouragement that follow are from a man and woman who committed themselves to the Lord first, then to one another and God's calling on their lives. They have taken their bruises, have had their breath knocked out of them, and have stumbled a time or two along the way. But it was in the prayer closet, individually and together, that they have been able to experience the joy set before them.

Denny Henderson
Pastor, Northlake Church
Lago Vista, Texas

Preface

I have known Dennis Henderson longer than anyone in my life. He is my older brother. As a child, he was my hero. He played football. I played football. When I was young I listened intently night after night as he preached a youth revival. At the end of the week, I trusted Jesus as my savior.

When I was in high school, wavering in my walk with Christ, my parents sent me to Arizona to be with Dennis as he preached at a youth camp. During that time, I surrendered my life fully to Christ again. In my college days, he suggested that I date Rosemary Brewer. She is now my wife of forty years. Countless times as a pastor, I have sought out Dennis for much-needed pastoral wisdom and perspective. In so many of the significant moments of my life God used Dennis to change my trajectory.

From the beginning of Strategic Renewal, Dennis has been involved at different levels. Today, I celebrate with joy that he is the National Director of The 6:4 Fellowship. His over 55 years of ministry bring a rare addition to our leadership team. We are brothers by family, brothers in Christ, and partners in ministry as he and Billie run hard to the finish line. Their lives challenge me to follow their steps into my future.

I wholeheartedly recommend this book for any couple desiring to grow in prayer together. It is chiseled from heartaches, disappointments, life-changing lessons, and faithfully praying together as a couple. I've had a front row seat watching Dennis and Billie serve Christ, His church, and one another. They have loved each other authentically and sacrificially for over a half century. This book will inspire you to seek God together – consistently, passionately, and enduringly.

Daniel Henderson
Founder & President – Strategic Renewal
Global Director – The 6:4 Fellowship

Introduction

Our twenty-eighth year of marriage was our twenty-seventh year of ministry. You would think that a pastor would have an exceptional prayer practice with his wife. We didn't. We prayed together, some. It was usually on the fly. For us, it took an awakening. Let me put it more honestly. It took a train wreck. Ministry had pushed our marriage down the line of priorities. Billie had been getting the scraps of time and focus. The one who is my first disciple was not being tenderly led in spiritual things. That crash, twenty-eight years ago, began a slow process of learning to pray together deeply and regularly. Prayer saved our marriage and ministry.

We now begin our marriage counseling with troubled couples with this question "How is your prayer time together?" One hundred percent have responded that they do not pray together. I ask pastors the same question in our private conversations, and over 80 percent give the same answer.

Why was it so hard for couples to establish a rhythm of intimate prayer? Over the years, we have seen surveys on that question. Schedules ranked high on the list. Like me, husbands left early for jobs and came home late and tired. It seemed like there just was not a slot in our day where we could drive a stake to pray.

Intimidation was another barrier. Physically strong husbands felt spiritually inferior when it came to prayer. Even I felt like Billie was the superior prayer person when we began. The list of hindrances could continue, but the most significant obstacle is the enemy who battles to destroy our marriages and the life God wants us to have.

BENEFITS OF PRAYING TOGETHER

It is said in the human psyche that one must understand the benefits to attempt anything challenging. Here are a few of the many benefits as I look back.

1 I discovered the joy of walking in obedience. My obedience in leading our prayer life has given me deep peace and satisfaction that I love God as I love my wife through prayer.

2. Praying together leads to vulnerability, humility, and dependence. As we grew in our prayer times, I found myself growing in being open and vulnerable. We found ourselves talking openly after prayer about issues that we usually would not discuss.

3. Praying together changed us. Together we sought God's direction, wisdom, and His face. We continued to grow in our dependence on Him and our confidence in Him. In the movie Shadowlands, C.S. Lewis says, "I pray because I can't help myself. I pray because I'm helpless. I pray because the need flows out of me all the time, waking and sleeping. It doesn't change God. It changes me." I became an authentic leader.

4. Praying together strengthens the bonds of trust, security, and intimacy. Billie has never felt more secure than she does today. Twenty-seven years of growing in prayer had brought about our most extraordinary moments of intimacy spiritually and physically, which cements our lives together as one flesh.

SOME SIMPLE IDEAS TO HELP YOU GET STARTED

We offer this book to help give couples an aid to help them get started in the habit of praying together. The daily topics are not a lengthy commentary on the subject. The topics are those we face in our marriages on a regular basis. They are merely jumping-off points to give you a start for prayer. We are sure that you will pray beyond the topic.

1. Set a time. It cannot be left up to "when you get time." You must select a time. Morning is our best time. Though I might have a 6:00 a.m. meeting, I will return home to pray with Billie at 8:00 a.m. Set your time.

2. Baby steps. Today, Billie and I will pray for 30 to 45 minutes each day. Somedays we will go for an hour. As you get started, take small steps. Five minutes consistently will turn to 10 or 20 minutes. However, your goal is not how long you pray. It is how often you pray. Praying often turns into a habit that you will not want to miss.

3. Pray short prayers. Some call this conversation prayer. Even today, I will drift if Billie prays for a lengthy time. We pray interactive prayers, which keep us focused.

4. Use the Bible to start the prayer. Take the passage at the top of the page each day and look for ways to acknowledge God. Look for His wisdom, goodness, promises in the passage. It is always an easy starter to allow God to begin our conversation through His word. We call this Scripture-feed prayer. The Scripture begins our thankfulness, pulls out our complaints and fears, and brings us to moments of worship. You may also take a psalm, read it together, and respond in prayer with what you see about God in the psalm. Then you may move on to the topic of the day.

Here is an example of how you may use Scripture of the day to help you start your prayer time together. One of the days, the prayer focus will be on unity in marriage. Two passage that begins the thoughts for that day are Amos 3:3 "Can two people walk together without agreeing on the direction?" The other is John 17:21 "I pray that they will all be one, just as you and I are one—as you are in me, Father, and I am in you." You may begin with thanking God that he is the God of all wisdom and thank Him for the reminder of how He wants us to be one. You may elaborate on that thought if you wish. Then when it comes to your request focus for that day, you may pray that you would have an agreement on an issue in your marriage that you may not be agreeing on. It could be a purchase, a job change, disciplining of your children. Here is a simple idea to help you.

"Father, you know we are trying to decide on the new job offer. We know we are one in you, and you desire for us to walk in unity. We acknowledge you are the God of wisdom. You know the future. You know we are not in agreement today. We surrender our wills. We put aside what we want individually. We sincerely want to do what will glorify you the most. May we set aside our thoughts right now. May we seek your pleasure. May you work in our minds, hearts, and circumstances to show us what we need to do. May we listen to Godly counsel. May we come to an agreement in this decision. We want to walk together as one, and we want your will to be."

The above prayer idea can be greatly improved. It is merely an idea of how to pray with God's Word being your prompting and guide.

5.   Don't misuse prayer. Sometimes prayer can used as tool to try to change each other. It can be subtle nudge for a mate to pray prayers that are shaded towards a change he or she wants in their mate. Prayer is not the time to do that. Therefore, we suggest using scripture to begin your prayer time. Let the Word of God set the tone and direction of your prayer time. Pray encouraging prayers for each other.

There is no more important activity in a marriage than prayer. A new house, car, gadget, clothes will not do for your marriage what prayer will do. Join us as we pray with you each day.

Dennis Henderson

PURPOSE

Dennis Henderson

The highest purpose of marriage is to display to the world the sacrificial love of Christ for his bride, the church.

Marriage is God's gift to us, designed to bring us joy and Him glory!

Then God said, "Let us make man *in our image, in our likeness*, and let them rule over the fish of the sea and the birds of the air, over the livestock, over all the earth, and over all the creatures that move along the ground. So, God created man in his own image, in *the image of God he created him; male and female* he created them." Genesis 1:26-27

Over the last forty-two years, I have discipled over six hundred men in small group settings with high accountability. In the study, I have a module on *purpose*. I begin the module by asking them to write out their life purpose statement. Ninety-nine percent of them look at me with a blank stare. We then spend the next five weeks working on a life statement. I do this because if men do not have a clear life purpose embedded in their minds, their jobs, friends, culture will design their life purpose. They then will be following the wrong path for their lives.

The same is true in marriage. A couple needs to have a marriage purpose statement written down. When Billie and I got married, we were eighteen years old. We were given no premarital preparation, and James Dobson had not written a book yet. The only thing we knew was I was going into ministry, and we wanted to serve God. At least, we knew we wanted God to be glorified in our lives. Beyond that, we were totally ignorant. Over the years, we finally developed a clear purpose for our marriage: our written marriage creed that gives us a statement of why we are married. It states the purpose of our marriage that includes children, money, possessions, prayer, and several other defining practices. It is the plumbline for us rather than being moved by every wind that blows in our environment.

Why is this important? Because the culture wants to shape your marriage, and Satan wants to destroy it. If we do not have a strong, clear, Biblical understanding of the purpose of marriage, then we can drift into a worldly shaped marriage with worldly values and practices with the tag of Christian marriage. So, let's nail down some truths for you to pray over and discuss in the days ahead.

• Marriage is for the purpose of reflecting God's image.

In Genesis 1:26, 27 above, the emphasis on "image" and "likeness." God creates "them" as a unit to reflect Him. It takes both a man and woman, in oneness, to truly reflect His image. When we criticize our spouse or foster division and competition, we reflect Satan's disunity and dishonoring God. On the other hand, when we recognize our purpose is to reflect the image of God, we are convicted by Holy Spirit when we don't meet that standard and are protected from hardening our hearts toward one another. This is why same-sex marriage is not a Biblical reflection of God's image.

• Marriage is for the purpose of glorifying God.

Marriage is not a separate part of our lives. It is ingrained in everything we do. Thus, in our conversations, financial management, activities, lifestyle, sexuality, usage of time, and all we do, we are to glorify, honor, reflect God. Marriage is the headwater for this. People should see Christ in all we do as a couple, a family. It should be clear why we exist as a couple. A house, job, possessions, a trophy wife, college-bound kids are not the purpose of marriage. These things might come in your marriage, but they are not the goal. The overarching and end goal is that two people following Jesus will bring Him glory through their being one in Christ and marriage

I Peter 2:12 "Live such good lives among the pagans that, though they accuse you of doing wrong, they may see your good deeds and glorify God on the day he visits us."

Colossians 3:17 "And whatever you do, whether in word or deed, do it all in the name of the Lord Jesus, giving thanks to God the Father through him."

• Marriage is a powerful picture of the Gospel

I have said for years that marriage is a powerful means of evangelism. As a couple lives out Jesus in their marriage, it reflects the Gospel. People observe two people committed to each other living a loving, consistent, caring, self-sacrificing manner with each other the picture of the Gospel is portrayed. Paul instructs on marriage in Ephesians 5:23-33. He explicitly teaches how the husband represents Christ through his love and care for the bride and presents her to God someday in the same way Christ presents his church to him, blameless. So, a great privilege, responsibility, and purpose of marriage shows the Gospel through our lives. In a society where marriages and relationships are disposable items, people should be asking you. "What is the reason and key to your enduring commitment to each other?" With fifty-six years of marriage, Billie and I have had many opportunities to share that Christ is the glue that keeps us together, which then opens doors to share the Gospel.

More could be said on this topic, but let's start with these foundational truths and pray that our marriages will fulfill God's purpose, which will satisfy us with joy, pleasure, and meaning. Join us this first day as we pray with you.

Join us in prayer for Day 1
at www.strategicrenewal.com/21days

PRIORITIES

Dennis Henderson

*"Ruthlessly eliminate hurry from your life.
Hurry is the enemy of the spiritual life." Dallas Willard*

Matthew 6:28 "why do you worry about clothes? See how the flowers of the field grow. They do not labor or spin. [29]Yet I tell you that not even Solomon in all his splendor was dressed like one of these. [30]If that is how God clothes the grass of the field, which is here today and tomorrow is thrown into the fire, will he not much more clothe you—you of little faith? [31]So do not worry, saying, 'What shall we eat?' or 'What shall we drink?' or 'What shall we wear?' [32]For the pagans run after all these things, and your heavenly Father knows that you need them. [33]But *seek first his kingdom* and his righteousness, and all these things will be given to you as well."

It would be an understatement to say we live busy, crowded, overextended lives today. Never in history have people lived at this pace. Our family vans are busier than a New York taxi with kids being rushed from one sport to another, to music, dance, art, and tutoring lessons. Meals are devoured as the van pulls out of the fast food. If there is not enough time to stop at the fast food, Mom just yells, "We have leftovers tonight, see what you can find in the pushed down in the seat cervices."

Then you have various other things that scream for your time and energy. Shortlist: Job, school activities, neighbors, service organizations, hobbies, and church. Everyone wants a piece of our time and, many times, money. I don't think I need to paint anymore on this canvas. You live the picture.

Our house is empty of kids, but our schedules are slower. Retirement has not come, and we see it or desire it nowhere on the horizon. However, I wonder what it would be like to live one hundred years ago. I believe life was slower, not less challenging, just slower. I try to imagine it was more peaceful, more centered on things that mattered.

With terms like margins, boundaries, overload, refocus, floating around, let me give you one more that might help you with your schedule. *Priorities*. I have told congregations for years, "Values are what we talk about, priorities are what we live." So it is crucial to pick the best choices on the smorgasbord before you.

Years ago, as I was studying Ephesians, I had one of those moments when the scriptures jumped out at me and became so clear. In Ephesians 5 and 6, Paul outlines the will of God. I will identify quickly what Billie and I teach in extended settings. Here is the short version and order of God's priorities for our lives.

1. God – 5:18-20

2. Spouse – 5:21-33

3. Children – 6:1-4

4. Vocation – 6:5-9

5. Ministry – 6:10-33

This is clear. It is in order. You adjust it, and you're in trouble. Yet, how often they are out of line. Vocation moves to the top. Children move to the top. For me, twenty-seven years of ministry at the top. I can testify that disaster can be at the door when the order is changed.

Let me give you what I tell couples all the time based on scripture, my failure, and hundreds of counseling sessions with couples. When we talk about priorities, we talk about time, energy, emotion, and money. This might not fly well, but here we go. Children are not the center of the home; no matter how cute you think princess might be, how much potential you think little athlete Andy has, most likely you have overrated them as you try to live your life through them. Here are the facts for high school boys.

In all pro sports, less than one percent of high school athletes make it to the pros in any sport. For example: football. About 1.1 million boys play football. Two hundred fifty five of them will make it to the NFL. So, here is the common sense I give to parents and my children whose kids are in sports and other activities. Unless NCAA Division 1 schools line up at your door for your child, stop driving your kids crazy and yourself with thousands of dollars and hours spent on them. They are not going to the pros. I love sports. I played sports. But we have gone off the rails with sports at all levels. So here is my advice to parents. Let your child play sports, one sport. Let them pick one artistic activity if they want but stop there. Stop all the travel teams. There go thousands of dollars a year. Spend your time with your family at home away from hurry, the godless culture. Spend time teaching the Word of God, having good conversations, actual family meals with cell phones turned off.

Where can we go next? Vocation. I can write a book on "The god of vocation." Read Ecclesiastes. Solomon gives excellent advice on the vanity of toil. Do not let the job control your life. Instead, work less and adjust your lifestyle. Don't move kids to number one or two. They are three. I told my kids, "I love you greatly, but I love your mother more. She is staying, and you are leaving someday."

One more, ministry and church. I am a pastor, but I tell you not to be at church multiple days and nights. Family comes before church.

I have to stop. So much more can be said in our insane society and schedules. The great command validates what I am saying. "Love God, Love your Neighbor." Matthew 22:37-38. Overloaded schedules diminish your time with God, your spouse, and your family.

Let's use the scriptures as our starting point today to think about our schedules and priorities.

Join us in prayer for Day 2
at www.strategicrenewal.com/21days

DAY 3

THE WORD OF GOD

Billie Henderson

"All Scripture is breathed out by God and profitable for teaching,
for reproof, for correction, and for training in righteousness,
that the man of God may be complete, equipped for every good work."
II Timothy 3:16-17

Years have passed since I was introduced to God. I was probably three years old. My mother taught me an evening prayer that many have repeated. "Now, I lay me down to sleep. I pray the Lord my soul to keep. If I should die before I wake, I pray the Lord my soul to take." Amazing it is that such a short and simple prayer could impact a young child! Though my parents were good people, they were infants in faith and faith-walking. I am still grateful that my mother taught me that prayer because it introduced me to the reality that God cares for me.

I never questioned God's existence. I attended church off and on still desiring to be right with this God who could keep my soul. As a teenager, my "someday" husband shared the Good News: Jesus died for me and loved me. I believed that and accepted Jesus into my life, which started me on a purposeful life to not only know this saving God but also serve Him. I was His.

Years later, married to a Christian leader, mother of four small children, I discovered that I had a great need in my life. It was not more activity; I was busy. My husband was zealously serving the Gospel, and I was busy at home. I was lonely and tired, disappointed and sad. One dark night, the soul thirsted and cried out to God for help. The still voice of the Holy Spirit impressed me to be more engaged in God's Word.

The following morning, as impoverished as we were, I went to the store and made the best investment of my life. I bought a college-ruled spiral notebook and set out to read and study God's Word. After the children were fast asleep, I prayed for guidance, closed my eyes, opened my Bible, and turned the pages. I stopped flipping through the pages and just pointed my finger somewhere on the page. I opened my eyes, read what my finger landed on, and snickered. My finger landed on Psalm 119:71. "It is good for me that I was afflicted, that I might learn your statutes." And so, in my "affliction," I began to take in the knowledge of God and experience a changed heart. So, the sun really did come out tomorrow!

Decades have passed, and my love for God's Word has only grown. Since that very dark, lonely night, God's Word has been shaping me as a wife, mother, grandmother, church leader, and friend. I have been challenged and taught to worship and pray. I now have years of journals stashed away that tell God's story in the life of one seeker. They are precious to me because they are MY records of God's teaching me His statutes in a personal way. These writings are not David's or some renowned Christian theologian's work. They are the testimony of God's Word at work in my life.

"How sweet are your words to my taste, sweeter than honey to my mouth! Through your precepts I get understanding; therefore, I hate every false way." Psalm 119:103 and 104

"If your law had not been my delight, I would have perished in my affliction. I will never forget your precepts, for by them you have given me life." Psalm 119:92-93

Jesus cautioned us, "...In the world you will have tribulation. But take heart; I have overcome the world." David was inspired to write these words in Psalm 119:165, "Great peace have those who love your law; nothing can make them stumble." I always need the truth from God's Word to keep me steady. You need it as well. As individuals or as a couple, we need truth to live as overcomers. Our attentiveness must be to love God and to know His truth. All of us need help in all kinds of seasons and situations. Let us commit to attending to the reading, studying, and submitting to the Word of God. His Word gives us life.

How can we love one another well? How can we give hope to one who is hurting? How can we forgive when we have been offended? How can we gain peace when life is hard? It is by the Word that our minds and hearts are enlarged. As God's people, single or married, let's pray that God and His Word would have priority in our lives.

Dennis and I not only spend individual time in God's Word and prayer, but we have practiced reading God's Word and letting it set the course for our daily times of praying together. God sets the tone and the direction for our prayer. The prayer is Scripture fed. As others have said, "Whoever begins the conversation sets the direction of the conversation." Every day is fresh and our hearts are in spiritual harmony. Without question, this practice has knitted our souls together and prepared us to live in God's will for our lives. The Scriptures and prayer have taught us how to navigate married life and face the challenges that surface: jobs, finances, parenting, forgiveness, fear and anxieties, sickness, relationships. We need God's wisdom and biblical direction to stay the course. So, dear ones, *"Devote yourselves to prayer, being watchful and thankful." Colossians 4:2.* Let God's Word feed your souls and lead you through this time of prayer together.

"His divine power has given us everything we need for life and godliness through our knowledge of him who called us by his own glory and goodness. Through these he has given us his very great and precious promises, so that through them you may participate in the divine nature and escape the corruption in the world caused by evil desires." 2 Peter 1:3-4

"You will show me the path of life; in Your presence is fullness of joy; at Your right hand are pleasures forevermore." Psalm 16:11 NKJV

Join us in prayer for Day 3
at www.strategicrenewal.com/21days

INTEGRITY

Billie Henderson

"Whoever walks in integrity walks securely, but he who makes his ways crooked will be found out." Proverbs 10:9

"The righteous who walks in his integrity – blessed are his children after him!" Proverbs 20:7

According to the dictionary, "integrity" is the quality of being honest and having strong moral principles or moral uprightness. Honesty and strong ethical principles are not prevalent in the American culture anymore. Our culture no longer celebrates the morally upright person. If anything, this person is an anomaly. One cannot be a student of the Word of God and not become sensitive to God's desire for His people to live blamelessly before others and before God Himself. One verse gives a warning, and the other verse suggests a blessing.

I try to be an upright person in my home and outside my home. Some years back, I had been reading through the Book of Proverbs. I desired to live by the principles written and so these thoughts were on my mind. At the time I thought I measured up pretty well with the standard set regarding a person's integrity. It's laughable to think that we are untouched by the subtlety of compromise, or should I say sin.

Being married to a pastor with four children and involved in church ministry, I was a busy woman. Phone calls were an interruption to my schedule, and I regarded many a call with disdain. One day I was swamped with ministry tasks and housework. I had limited time to meet my deadlines. The phone rang more than enough times, and I was bothered to say it mildly. The phone rang again, and out of the expectations of others, I answered it. The person on the other end talked endlessly while I silently simmered. In my frustration and "creativity," I asked one of my daughters to go ring the doorbell. "Oh, I am so sorry. Someone is at my front door. I will get back to you." So, I took care of that call. Someone WAS outside my front door ringing the doorbell, but it was my daughter. I tended to my chores, and the Word I read began to speak to my dishonest ways. At the conclusion of the day, I gathered the children and asked for their forgiveness. I had been openly dishonest before my children...they saw my crooked ways. Well, that was humbling.

I surmise the next questions are: Do I walk with integrity before the Lord? Am I willing to respond in complete obedience to Him? Will I forgive others just like He forgives me? Will I love those who are hard to love? Will I be a person of reconciliation or ignore situations that might be hard to confront? Will I tell the truth even though it might cost me something?

Years ago, I worked in a mortgage company in Dallas, Texas. We were about to move to a new ministry in California. My husband had already moved ahead of the family because my twin daughters had two more months until their high school graduation, and I still needed to sell our house. I had already taken my vacation days at work. Many others took sick days and went shopping or just stayed home. Of course, these people were paid for their time off. I, too, had many sick days coming, but I wasn't sick. So, I went to my manager and asked if I could have that Friday off. I told him that I knew I could have called in sick, but I wanted to be honest with him. He said, "I appreciate that, Billie, but you have used up all of your vacation time. I will let you off on Friday, but I won't pay you." Immediately, I thought of all the lunch hours that I had not taken to get some document out and never put it on my timesheet. He knew that I did that frequently. He knew that I could have been paid had I just called in sick. To be honest, it didn't seem fair. Honesty cost me money, but I kept my integrity and moral standard. There are times when integrity will cost us something, but in return, we gain God's approval which is worth more than our loss.

As you pray today, confess where you may have compromised your integrity. Ask the Holy Spirit to help you guard your integrity so that your behavior validates your testimony and adorns the Gospel that you share with others.

"Blessed are those whose way is blameless, who walk in the law of the Lord." Psalm 119:1

"He who walks in integrity walks securely, … ". Proverbs 10:9a

"But you have upheld me because of my integrity, and set me in your presence forever." Psalm 41:12

Join us in prayer for Day 4
at www.strategicrenewal.com/21days

DAY 5

GRATITUDE

Billie Henderson

"Not that I am speaking of being in need, for I have learned in whatever situation I am to be content. I know how to be brought low, and I know how to abound. In any and every circumstance, I have learned the secret of facing plenty and hunger, abundance and need."
Philippians 4:11-12

We have four children. Our middle two are twin girls. When they were around eight years old, I purchased two cute dresses on sale. When the girls were born, the pediatrician had suggested that if we decided to dress them alike, try at best, make the clothing different colors so each child could develop individual personalities with personal preferences. Having heard his advice, I tried to comply. I was excited to surprise the girls with new dresses. One dress was blue, and the other dress was red. So, I handed them each a dress and was disappointed in the reaction of one of my daughters. She didn't like the colors! She began to cry. In my grown-up perspective, I thought they should have been grateful that I even bought them dresses. The next hour was quite dramatic. I was trying to explain that gifts should be received with gratitude. Her reaction caused us to miss a party that would have been enjoyable.

When I rehearse that scene, I know God must often be disappointed in me. Things happen in life, and rather than being grateful, I grumble. He is good. He gives what I need, I know that, but I am guilty of not always receiving what He gives with a grateful heart.

I was an only child. Growing up in my father's home was quite an adventure. An adventure that I did not want to experience. Before I graduated high school, I had been to over 21 schools. I can still hear my dad's encouragement, "Bill, just think of all the new friends you will make." I didn't want to make new friends. I liked the friends that I had. Life was filled with new homes, new neighborhoods, new friends. Over time, I learned to accept the situation, but I was not grateful. I reiterated to my mother, "When I get married, we are going to buy a house and live in that house until we die!" As life happens, I have lived in 28 houses with my prince!

Looking back, I have learned to appreciate God's sovereignty and even be grateful. He knew that I would need to learn the art of flexibility and to grow in gratitude and contentment. I made many new friends. Some of these friends have become my mentors or prayer partners. They have shared life with me, and I am so blessed to know them. I have lived in large homes and small homes. I loved some of our homes, but I learned always to be grateful for a roof over my head. I definitely do not have deep roots in any place. As a citizen of heaven, I suppose that is a good way to view life on earth. God used my childhood to prepare me for my adulthood. I have not missed the party!

As a woman who deeply longs for security, God has trained me to accept what comes my way. I may struggle initially, but I quickly accept new situations. Are we ever prepared for hard times? That is always a challenge. Almost three years ago, my husband suffered a spinal stroke. It is an extremely rare condition. Initially, he was paralyzed from the waist down, with the future uncertain of any change. Almost immediately, I felt the peace that God gives. In a surreal way, I was grateful knowing that God was with us and that He would strengthen us as we faced our uncertain future. It was God's sovereignty that I trusted. I can't explain it. God gifted me peace, of which I am so grateful. Like Paul, I was learning throughout my life to walk the road that was before me and to trust God for provision. I am not super-spiritual nor holier than anyone. God's workmanship in my life was and is on display. By the way, as of this writing, my husband can walk, although he battles constant pain. He has always been a warrior. I am so very proud of his fight! We are grateful that God sustains us even through life's challenges.

As I write and ponder my upbringing, I am grateful for what I learned. I learned not to be so shy. I learned how to adapt to differing environments and let go of the past to embrace the future. God was preparing me to live in the present and accept all kinds of people and situations to serve Him in the local church.

As you turn to prayer today, be grateful in your circumstances, knowing that God is present. Thank Him for His provision and protection, His power and wisdom being confident in His character, His love, and His sovereignty. Be grateful for the big and little things He is doing to create the image of Christ in you and your marriage. It is about His glory.

"Now may the Lord of peace himself give you peace at all times in every way. The Lord be with you all." II Thessalonians 3:16

"In everything give thanks; for this is the will of God in Christ Jesus for you." I Thessalonians 5:18 NASB

"He turns a desert into pools of water, a parched land into springs of water." Psalm 107:35

Join us in prayer for Day 5
at www.strategicrenewal.com/21days

DAY 6

FORGIVENESS

Billie Henderson

"Be kind to one another, tenderhearted, forgiving one another, as God in Christ forgave you." Ephesians 4:32

"Then Peter came up and said to him, 'Lord, how often will my brother sin against me, and I forgive him: As many as seven times?' Jesus said to him, 'I do not say seven times, but seventy-seven times?'" Matthew 18:21-22

"You have heard that it was said, 'You shall love your neighbor and hate you enemy.' But I say to you, Love your enemies and pray for those who persecute you, so that you may be sons of your Father who is in heaven. ... " Matthew 5:43-45a

"If we confess our sins, he is faithful and just to forgive us our sins and to cleanse us from all unrighteousness." I John 1:9

"Forgiveness is an act of the will, and the will can function regardless of the temperature of the heart." Corrie Ten Boom

"Forgiveness doesn't make the other person right; it makes you free." Stormie Omartian

Forgiveness is a driving theme in the Word of God. As humans, we need God's forgiveness for our rebellion against Him. We are instructed to forgive others who might have offended us or hurt us in some way. As humans, we need to learn how to forgive ourselves when we have not met our expectations according to our value system of behavior. From the garden of Eden onward, God purposed to help us obtain the forgiveness we needed from our sins against Him and our sins against others. The Cross is a precious gift that frees us from the guilt of our sins and the repercussions of not being forgiving toward ourselves and others. Both those who forgive and those who receive forgiveness reap great benefits.

I was nine years old. My playmate accused me of something that I did not do. She lied about me to my mother. I loudly and vehemently protested to my mother, who quickly sent me to my room as a punishment. It was a late summer afternoon, and I could hear all of the other children playing outside. I was miserable. It was unfair. I was innocent of the accusation. My mother had not listened to me and had believed a lie. But, as all nine-year-old girls might do, I sat on my bed and cried. Not only could I not play, but my mother said that I would not get to have some watermelon that night when she and dad enjoyed their treat. I had so looked forward to that watermelon. This just couldn't be happening. Darn! In some ways, it seems silly now, but that watermelon was a big deal then! AND my mother had not believed my defense. An hour or so passed, and my mother walked into the bedroom. She sat down on the bed. Evidently, my other playmates told my mother that I was not guilty of the accusation. She said that she was sorry and asked me to forgive her. Yet, because of the way I protested, I still would not get to have the watermelon that night. So, I was free to go back outside and resume playing with the other children. Being a sensitive, only child, I still feel the sting from that episode.

I also learned two important lessons about the issue of forgiveness. First, my mother's acknowledgment of her wrong freed her from her guilt, and it freed me from my shame and hurt. We both received what we needed: forgiveness. Second, we could leave my bedroom with our relationship restored and the weight of our wrong actions being lifted from us. Forgiveness brought restoration on so many levels for daughter and mother.

Many years have passed since that incident, and I have had more opportunities to exercise my will to forgive. Haven't we all? Our choice to forgive or not forgive affects others and our wellness. Jesus insists that forgiveness is a choice of will and that forgiving is a repetitive action. Forgiveness is not a one-time choice; it is a continual process with no limits. As disciples of Christ, we are to emulate His life. The power that resurrected Christ dwells within us, so we can forgive as He forgives whether our forgiveness is sought or not. There is no other option.

Two people make a couple. Each has different personalities, histories, perspectives, and a host of other possible conflicting distinctions, which presents many opportunities to learn this process of forgiving. On occasion, Dennis withdraws into his own world. He seems troubled. As a woman, I always want to fix it. How many times have I asked him what was bothering him? Perhaps I could help him resolve an issue. I was generally told that it was nothing to concern myself with and just to leave it alone. I felt like he had something against me. Note that I used the word felt. There was a barrier between us, and I resented him for not allowing me to make it right. Over the years, I now understand that he has gone into his "man-cave." When he has come to terms with his conflict, he will come out, and life will resume normalcy. I learned that the residual hurt that I felt was causing resentment to take root in my emotions. The only solution was to forgive him for leaving me out of his struggles so that I could be free of my hurt and free to love without conditions. Perhaps, this is a common occurrence in marriage, but certainly it has been a tutor in my life. Forgiveness, whether needed or asked for, is a natural pattern of behavior for me as a result

Being a pastor's wife, I have had many opportunities to be blind-sighted by intentional or unintentional offenses. Some years ago, I was deeply hurt by the judgment and criticism from a family in one of our churches. My husband and I had made a ministry decision that was rational to us. He would represent us at a funeral of someone neither of us had met, and I would fill a ministry gap to help someone complete their responsibility at the church. Both activities were at the same time. My absence at the funeral became the topic of conversation at the meal after the service. When I heard how offended the group felt, I immediately addressed it. I went to them and asked for their forgiveness. They denied taking any offense, so I left thinking all was settled. As the enemy would have it, they were still offended and held resentment in their hearts toward me for many years. Some of the family even left the church and denied themselves ministry opportunities in our growing church. I was devastated at the time. However, they had a choice to forgive, just as I had a choice to go to them and ask for their mercy. It was a very sad time for me. Years have passed and I came to the realization that I had done nothing wrong; I had obeyed the instruction from God's Word. Their poor response denied true reconciliation and certainly did not glorify God and the Gospel. I believe I was released from any burden of guilt and was free to love them in their immaturity.

To live an unhindered life, has meant that I must forgive quickly, or I will squelch opportunities to love as Christ loved. My prayers will be hindered if I don't confront the offenses. I want to live in the freedom of Christ, don't you? So, as you pray today, ask the Holy Spirit to reveal any unresolved offense that might be causing resentment or bitterness to be taking root in your soul or another's soul. Perhaps you have done something wrong, and you haven't forgiven yourself. God encourages us to confess our sins to Him and He will forgive us completely so that we can live an unburdened life. As you pray, be open to the Holy Spirit's voice. Do you need to release resentment? Do you need to forgive? Do you need to be forgiven? David wrote, *"Blessed is he whose transgressions are forgiven, whose sins are covered. Blessed is the man whose sin the Lord does not count against him and in whose spirit is no deceit." (Psalm 32:1-2)*

Join us in prayer for Day 6
at www.strategicrenewal.com/21days

DAY 7

COMMUNICATION

Dennis Henderson

*"Communication in a marriage is like oxygen to life.
Without it...it dies."*

*"A major ingredient in communication is time....
a lot of time." Dennis Henderson*

"Hear what they are saying, not what you are thinking."
Dennis Henderson

Psalm 19:14 "Let the words of my mouth and the meditation of my heart be acceptable in your sight, O Lord, my rock and my redeemer."

Proverbs 25:11 "A word fitly spoken is like apples of gold in a setting of silver.

[12]Like a gold ring or an ornament of gold is a wise reprover to a listening ear.

[13]Like the cold of snow in the time of harvest is a faithful messenger to those who send him; he refreshes the soul of his masters."

Colossians 4:6. "Let your speech always be gracious, seasoned with salt, so that you may know how you ought to answer each person."

Two people living together brings an inherent measure of stress, conflict, and disagreement. We need to keep in mind that we are the downline of Adam and Eve. Ever since the fall of Adam and Eve, interpersonal relationships have been flawed and have taken an extreme amount of work for people to interact without some degree of misunderstanding. Words can be at the top of the list in determining the quality of a relationship.

Because Billie and I grew up in dysfunctional homes and yelling rang throughout our homes, we decided that would never take place with us. My four grown kids can verify that they have never heard us yell at each other. We have never had a major argument. We have had disagreements, but never to the point of yelling or going off the rails. Well, I have slammed a door or two on my way out but never have allowed our conversations to escalate to the point where my words or actions were threatening. We are proud of that one piece in our marriage. However, there are other chinks in my communication armor.

Looking back over our fifty-six years of marriage, I painfully recall the times I did not choose my words wisely. I said them when my mind was on other things or irritated by something at church or the kids. I spoke too quickly, and the words came out harshly. They were cutting. I could immediately see the hurt in her eyes. I have always cherished Billie and never wanted to be mean or treat her like I watched some of my stepfathers treat my mother.

A word, sentence, or conversation that is not thoughtfully chosen can cause significant damage. The sad part of words once the words are out, the harm is done. The comments are not erased. In James 3:1-12, we are reminded of the evil the tongue can possess. James says it can be like a deadly poison or wildfire. In contrast, Proverbs 25 speaks of words as apples of gold, rings of gold, and cold snow that refreshes the soul.

After establishing who we are in Christ in the first three chapters of Ephesians and our unity in Christ, Paul begins in 4:17 to tell us in practical ways how we live out our life in Christ. It does not take long for him to address our words. In verse 29, he instructs, "Don't use foul or abusive language. Let everything you say be good and helpful so that your words will be an encouragement to those who hear them." (NLT). This is a passage we all need to read and often repeat as we are caught up in the whirlwind of our daily schedules.

We must remind ourselves regularly what Emerson Eggerichs, in his book "Love and Respect," calls "pink and blue ears." What may be a joke for a man could be a piercing put down for a woman. When I speak to Billie, I must keep in mind that I am not in the locker room with a bunch of guys jesting. She hears through "pink" ears. Paul in Ephesians 5:25 tells husbands to love their wives as Christ loved the church. The love of Christ for us is always with words that nourishes us, comforts us, protects us.

Paul concludes in Ephesians 5:31 the two significant needs of wives and husbands are love and respect. Words of love are tender, kind, uplifting, endearing. Words of respect tell of accomplishment, significance, gratitude, affirmation.

Could words be an area that you need to pray about today? Do you need to stop and ask each for forgiveness for words recently spoken? As you pray with us, let's have ears open to the Holy Spirit concerning the conversations we have. Join us as we ask God for the words of our mouth and the meditations of our hearts to be acceptable to Him and pleasing to our spouse.

Ephesians 4:29 "Let no corrupting talk come out of your mouths, but only such as is good for building up, as fits the occasion, that it may give grace to those who hear."

Join us in prayer for Day 7
at www.strategicrenewal.com/21days

DAY 8

UNITY

Billie Henderson

"Therefore a man shall leave his father and his mother and hold fast to his wife, and they shall become one flesh." Genesis 2:24

"Do two walk together, unless they have agreed to meet?" Amos 3:3

"...giving thanks always and for everything to God the Father in the name of our Lord Jesus Christ, submitting to one another out of reverence for Christ." Ephesians 5: 20-21

"...walk in a manner worthy of the calling to which you have been called, with all humility and gentleness, with patience, bearing with one another in love, eager to maintain the unity of the Spirit in the bond of peace." Ephesians 4:1-3

"Finally, all of you, have unity of mind, sympathy, brotherly love, a tender heart, and a humble mind." I Peter 3:8

"The goal of marriage is not to think alike, but to think together."
– Unknown

Marriage is a partnership between two people with differing personalities, family histories, worldviews, and ways of behavior. We have prayed over the last few days on many aspects of marriage. Unity is a powerful and necessary component in marriage and foundational in the union between the spouses. Clearly, the Bible states that each spouse must hold fast to the other out of reverence to Christ and the Gospel.

The perspective in Christian marriage is vital. Christian marriage presents the power of the Gospel as the couple shares the purpose of God's rule in the marriage. Spouses retain separate identities but unite in the Spirit's plan for their lives as a couple. There must be a mutual commitment to God's glory. Charles Spurgeon was a nineteenth-century preacher. He and his wife, Susannah, were married for thirty-six years. They battled through illness, depression, and tremendous criticism from the national press. Charles writes a poem to his wife. They shared the same view on the sovereignty of God believing, that God's glory would guide them through tough seasons. Charles wrote:

> *"Though he who chose us all worlds before*
>
> *Must rein in our hearts alone.*
>
> *We fondly believe that we shall adore*
>
> *Together before his throne."*

They fixed their eyes on His glory and not their own. Perspective seems to come before practice.

The Bible sets the prerequisite for unity. When the couple unites, each must emotionally leave their parent's home and commit totally to their new spouse. They begin to serve one another by looking out for the interests and desires of the other. They must both choose to trust God. They must learn to have honest conversations as they build a friendship.

After 56 years of marriage, we have experienced repercussions from not being united in decisions. We also experienced great peace and unity when we trusted God to guide us in decision-making. Some years ago, a close associate of my husband and a family friend experienced a financial crisis. Having exhausted his resources, he asked Dennis for help. Without discussing or praying with me, Dennis made an emotionally-driven decision. He co-signed a banknote for a loan to keep our friend financially solvent. Unfortunately, I was unaware of his actions. Months later, the banknote came due. Our friend was still financially impoverished and could not pay off the debt.

We were then responsible. We owned the debt. At that juncture, Dennis told me what he had done and that I would need employment to help pay the loan. I found a job, but it caused some strain in our marriage and family on many levels. Time passed, and we went to another church. The profit gained after selling our house settled the debt. We were now unable to buy a house in our new community. I will say that God used the situation to train us in better financial management and the need for unity in prayer when making decisions. Working in the secular marketplace opened my eyes anew to the world's ways and the world's need for the Gospel. God did not waste the experience, but it was a difficult time in our lives. I battled resentment and bitterness in my heart at the unfairness. I learned a new lesson in the healing power of forgiveness.

There have been other occasions when we prayed together and came to the same conclusion. We were offered an opportunity to join a mission organization, and Dennis would become the national director. To be honest, we had surrendered our lives to international mission work during our college years. We just wanted to fulfill whatever God desired for us. Simultaneously, a church in California had contacted Dennis about becoming the lead pastor. The location of the ministry was not our concern. We were willing to serve anywhere. The dilemma was the kind of calling and preparedness of Dennis. We were excited about both posts. So we decided to fast and pray and spent one night in a hotel to discuss both ministries' pros and cons. In the morning, we revealed our conclusions.

I believed that my husband was a prepared pastor, not a manager of pastors. He was still conflicted. I went to work and prayed for God's revelation. After spending another night in prayer, Dennis was satisfied with the direction he should follow. He loved the "sheep." He was a pastor. The decision was clear, and it was a great decision. The new church ministry was joyful and fruitful. If my husband had decided to join the mission agency, I would have followed willingly. He has the head leadership role in the marriage and, as a surrendered woman and wife, I would have followed his lead and trusted God to provide. There is the mutual respect in marriage, and there are defined biblical roles that God has put in the Scriptures. Prayer fostered respect and unity.

Training children in the family is vital and all-consuming. If ever unity is needed, it is in parenting. A united front is paramount, so there need to be discussions on the boundaries and to create a family code for living together. Not only is prayer powerful, but a genuine appreciation for differing views can be eye-opening. Remember, releasing your own experience growing up, may help you quickly forge a new and better path forward in your parenting skills together. Unity before the children is life-giving.

Unity is fostered by each partner having a spirit of humility, gentleness, patience, and loving forbearance. Unity means we serve our mates. Partners do not respond in anger when challenged agendas or wrongs are committed. There are many ways of doing things, so there must be a willingness to listen to one another.

"And above all these put on love, which binds everything together in perfect harmony." Colossians 3:14

Jesus prayed in John 17:22-23. "The glory that you have given me I have given to them, that they may be one even as we are one, I in them and you in me, that they may become perfectly one, so that the world may know that you sent me and loved them even as you loved me."

As you pray today, ask the Spirit to show you where there may be a breach in the unity of your marriage. Ask Him to change your desires and surrender them for the sake of unity. Thank God for His love and power, lived out in your marriage, allowing you the blessing of bringing Him glory and putting His Gospel on display to your children and the people to whom you have impact. End the time with an expression of gratitude toward one another and renew your commitment to be united in purpose and service.

Join us in prayer for Day 8
at www.strategicrenewal.com/21days

FEAR AND ANXIETY

Billie Henderson

"…for God gave us a spirit not of fear but of power and love and self-control." I Peter 1:7

"God is our refuge and strength, a very present help in trouble. Therefore we will not fear though the earth gives way, though the mountains be moved into the heart of the sea, though the mountains tremble at its swelling." Psalm 46:1-3

"When I am afraid, I put my trust in you. In God, whose word I praise, in God I trust; I shall not be afraid. What can flesh do to me?" Psalm 56:3-4

"The presence of fear does not mean you have no faith. Fear visits everyone. But make your fear a visitor and not a resident." Max Lucado

"Where does your security lie? Is God your refuge, your hiding place, your stronghold, your shepherd, your counselor, your friend, your redeemer, your Savior, your guide? If He is, you don't need to search any further for your security." Elizabeth Elliot

Much in our world can certainly cause us to succumb to fear and anxiety. There are wars, famines, natural disasters, crime in the cities, illnesses, relationship struggles, finances, job losses, and the unknowns. Most of the anxiety we face is in our heads. Our brains use fear to prepare us to face or escape danger or deal with stressful situations. In the United States, over 40 million adults are diagnosed with anxiety disorders and depression brought on by stress and fear. Not only does the brain engage in fear, but our bodies even react to the stress. The body may have an increased heart rate, sweating, rapid breathing, trembling, tiredness, restlessness, and trouble concentrating. Fear cripples us and is used by the enemy of our souls to control our emotions and decisions so that the weight of the "what ifs" overwhelms us and turns our focus from God to our circumstances. Faith is stifled.

Fear is not from God. He gives us the power to overcome fear and the ability to maintain self-control. That power is readily available, but we have to choose to act upon it. We must decide not to let fear control us, to instead intentionally fill our minds with God's Word, to pray and replace what is in our thoughts. We can guard our hearts in this way. We can trust God's Word, which is life, and it will soothe our souls. We must discipline our minds repeatedly until faith is more engrained in our lives than the fears that threaten our peace. Such disciplines must be repetitive until faith naturally comes forth when fear releases its tentacles into our souls.

As a young girl, I can recall times and again when I would hear a siren outside the school windows when sitting at my desk in school to be overtaken by fear. My first thought was the welfare of my mother at home. Had something happened to her? Was the house on fire? I lost focus on the teacher because I was overwhelmed at the possible loss that I was going to experience. My mother was my world, my anchor, my supporter. I expected to be called to the school office to be told the dreadful news. The foreboding was so dark. When no one came for me, I was even more engulfed with the fear that no one knew I was her daughter and she was alone. Such occurrences were many.

As I grew into adulthood, I was gripped again with the same dread only now it concerned the loss of my husband or one of my children. I had accepted Christ as my Savior by adulthood, but I was not consistent in Bible reading, study, and prayer. I was defenseless with the most powerful of weapons so nearby.

One night I was leading a Bible study in my home. My daughter had just left for work in another town, so she commuted on a busy highway where the truckers ruled the roads. The ladies had their coffee and gathered in the den when sirens started blaring outside. I quickly excused myself and ran outside to see if one of the big trucks had hit my daughter. My heart pounded, and fear gripped my soul. The ladies saw the fear in my countenance and ran out the front door behind me to see what was the matter. It was so humbling to share with them the battle I had with fear.

I wish I could tell you that I don't battle this kind of fear. I still do, but I do believe in God's sovereignty and His promises. I can recall His faithfulness over the years and trust in His will and purposes, for I have committed myself to the reading of God's Word, memorizing it, and learning the power of prayer. It is comforting now that when life threatens me, I may face fear initially, but very quickly, I find my faith takes over, and I trust in God to help me meet any circumstance that will be presented. It is my natural response for the most part now because self-control has become a reality.

When my husband had his spinal stroke, and we faced the unknown future, the faith in me kept me steady. God had seen us through many storms, and I had the confidence that He would do it again. How? I had no idea, but I knew that He would. He did! God is our present help, and we can trust in Him. He is faithful to keep His Word, my friends.

As you pray today, you, too, may be facing a crisis that is causing fear to override your faith. Look at the verses at the opening of the reading. Read them out loud. Make them personal. Thank God for His help and ask the Holy Spirit to settle your soul and train you in renewing your mind through God's Word. Trust in God's power to sustain you. Encourage yourself with this exhortation: *"He gives power to the faint, and to him who has no might he increases strength."* *(Isaiah 40:29)* Jesus spoke into our fear when he said, *"In the world, you will have tribulation (trouble). But take heart; I have overcome the world."* Thank God for the victory He has provided for you as you release your fear to His control and then rest in His promise. Encourage one another in these truths, my friends. God keeps His Word.

Join us in prayer for Day 9
at www.strategicrenewal.com/21days

CONTENTMENT

Dennis Henderson

Contentment always eludes those who do not count themselves blessed for what they already have.

Eccles 5:10 "He that loveth silver shall not be satisfied with silver; nor he that loveth abundance increase: this is also vanity."

Proverbs 27:21 "Death and Destruction are never satisfied, and neither are human eyes."

1 Timothy 6:6 "But godliness with contentment is great gain, ⁷for we brought nothing into the world, and we cannot take anything out of the world. ⁸But if we have food and clothing, with these we will be content."

Twice in three short verses, Paul urges us to be content. Contentment plays a considerable role in a marriage. Never being satisfied with your station in life can impact every area of your marriage. Contentment relates to comparison, covetousness, and competition.

Comparing can be destructive when you compare things that our culture values as important. For example, the square footage of a house, the make of a car, the brand names of clothes, the airbrushed and surgically improved physical beauty are all things that are never helpful. Paul reminds us not to compare with others. 1 Corinthians 4:7 When we compare ourselves to others, we agree with the enemy's plans for our lives. Comparison is the thief of joy and the stretcher of truth. Comparison never leads to contentment. Those who compare and live with discontentment are noted as fools in the Bible.

The apostle Paul gives his testimony on contentment Philippians 4:11 "I am not saying this because I am in need, for I have learned to be *content* whatever the circumstances. 12 I know what it is to be in need, and I know what it is to have plenty. I have learned the secret of being content in any and every situation, whether well fed or hungry, whether living in plenty or in want. 13 I can do all this through him who gives me strength". In 2 Corinthians 11:23-28, Paul tells of his circumstances during his life. It is worth reading as you discover a life of incredible suffering. Yet, he was content. Why? Because he did not define his life by his circumstances. He described his life by his belief in the sovereignty of God. He had a deep trust in God, knowing his situation was used for the betterment of God's purpose. He found his strength in Christ. So, let's establish a definition for contentment: Contentment is a deep satisfaction knowing what God has given us is for His goodwill in our lives. Contentment is a choice that makes all the difference in our happiness together.

Adam and Eve were not satisfied with paradise. They listened to a lie from Satan that more would be better. We are hard-wired to want more. Wanting more of the world's offerings, changes in our spouse, better things can bring significant damage to our marriages. We are surrounded with lies of more daily from social media, advertisements, and conversations in the office and even our friends. John gives us wonderful advice in

I John 2:15 "Do not love the world or the things in the world. If anyone loves the world, the love of the Father is not in him. [16]For all that is in the world—the desires of the flesh and the desires of the eyes and pride of life—is not from the Father but is from the world. [17]And the world is passing away along with its desires, but whoever does the will of God abides forever."

How can we nourish contentment?

- See our marriage for the purpose of God to be shown in all our circumstances.

- Live with thankfulness as it takes the focus off me and places it on God and what is best in others.

- Thankfulness is powerful because it is a step of obedience. In every situation, Christians are expressly instructed to give thanks – express gratefulness. Now, that's difficult to do when our eyes are on ourselves. But, when we are focused on the purposes of God in our lives, and the eyes of our hearts are on Him, suddenly giving thanks amid circumstances we do not like has meaning far beyond how we feel. 1 Thessalonians 5:18 says, "In everything give thanks for this is the will of God in Christ Jesus concerning you." So that you and I express gratefulness – even during the bad stuff – is God's will.

- Thankfulness is powerful because it comes with a promise. When we are discontent, we lack peace in our lives. Philippians 4:6 says, "Be anxious for nothing; but in everything by prayer and supplication with thanksgiving let your request be made known unto God and the peace of God, which passes all understanding, will guard your hearts and minds in Christ Jesus." Peace . . . contentment. That's a great promise!

Our spouses aren't perfect, but last time I checked, neither is that guy I saw in the mirror this morning. Contentment is never found if we focus on our spouse's shortcomings rather than on the many things about them that we can be genuinely grateful for, not to mention the many mercies and blessings we receive from God daily.

Today as you pray together, do you have anything to be grateful? Let God know. And then, let your spouse know something about them which you are thankful. Praying with gratitude will lead you to what you have is enough, and that will cultivate contentment.

Join us in prayer for Day 10
at www.strategicrenewal.com/21days

DAY 11

FINANCES

Dennis Henderson

*"As base a thing as money often is, yet it can be transmuted
into everlasting treasure. It can be converted into food for the hungry
and clothing for the poor. It can keep a missionary actively winning
lost men to the light of the gospel and thus transmute itself into
heavenly values. Any temporal possession can be turned into everlasting
wealth. Whatever is given to Christ is immediately touched with
immortality." A.W. Tozer*

*"A man could have all the money in all the banks in all the world
and be worth nothing so far as God is concerned if he were still living
to and for himself"! Ian Thomas*

*It's about time we stopped buying things we don't need with money we
don't have to impress people we don't like. Adrian Rogers*

It has been a constant in marriage surveys that finances will be one
of the top five conflicts in a marriage. Another constant in marriage information is that finances are the leading three causes of divorce. Many go into marriage with instructions on the management
of money. It would be towards the top of the list of things Billie and
I had no idea about when we got married. We did understand the
principle of tithing. From the first day of our marriage, that was

never a question. We never missed a tithe through college, which we paid for ourselves, raising four kids, all having orthodontics, and the regular bills of life. However, we did stack up debt due to my ignorance and impulsiveness. Even today, with all the knowledge and practice of good stewardship in my life, I try to stay out of Cabela's or any other outdoor store. In our forties, I finally got serious about living debt-free. It took us almost eight years to clear our debt caused by my unwise decision. For the last twenty-five years, we have lived debt-free. Today, we live on a cash basis, have a healthy savings account, our current house we bought with cash, and any vehicle will be purchased with cash. All the time, we have been able to give hundreds of thousands to God's work. I say this not to boast, for it has indeed been God's blessings. I say this because debt-free living removes one of the tensions in our home that many live with daily. Practicing Biblical principles of stewardship brings peace, joy, and even intimacy to your marriage.

Today, I do not write to give a course on money management. You can find plenty of material by Dave Ramsey, Randy Alcorn, Howard Dayton, and many others on this topic. I want to come alongside you today as a couple draws this to a significant area of prayer while noting a few principles to help you. First, never make a financial decision without praying together for some time. Second, always agree on your finances obey the scriptures. Third, be aware that Satan desires for you to be saddled with debt and to allow it to spark some pretty good disagreements. Can I remind you what the world says: Money will make you happy, possessions make you secure, credit is available with easy payments. Well, all of those statements oppose scripture.

I remind you that you were joined as one flesh. Consequently, most Biblical financial advisors and I would not recommend separate financial accounts. This sets you up for "his and hers" money rather than ours. Meet regularly to discuss your finances and ensure there are no hidden items. Distinguish needs, wants, and consumerism. Needs are essentials. Wants are things beyond needs. Consumerism is spending based on impulse, attractive marketing. It is found in greed and wanting more.

If you have children at home, teach them about the wise stewardship of money. Teach them early how to work and earn money. Break the entitlement mentality that is running ramped among the millennials down to generation z. No, they do not need the latest video game, iPhone, $300 pair of tennis shoes, or $150 pair of jeans. Model to them giving. From the early days of our children's lives, we taught tithing and sacrificial giving to them and shared what we gave to God each week. We wanted them to learn generosity and trust God with us for daily needs rather than a piece of plastic. Do not let their greedy little hearts run the home.

Today, may the Holy Spirit remind us that we cannot serve two masters. Billie and I continue to pray about purchases, giving, our dependence on God, and not the artificial security of money. We never want our possessions to possess us. What do you need to bring to God today about finances? What or who rules your hearts. God has given you an income. He wants you to live within it. This might mean that you need to ask God to direct you to some needed help.

Join us in prayer for Day 11
at www.strategicrenewal.com/21days

EXPECTATIONS

Billie Henderson

"And now, O Lord, for what do I wait? My hope is in you."
Psalm 39:7

"For God alone, O my soul, wait in silence, for my hope is from him."
Psalm 62:5

"For I know the plans I have for you, declares the LORD, plans for welfare and not for evil, to give you a future and a hope."
Jeremiah 29:11

"For all the promises of God find their Yes in him. That is why it is through him that we utter our Amen to God for his glory."
II Corinthians 1:20

"Real faith believes God can, and expects that He will, but trusts Him even if He doesn't." Jerrid Wilson

"Disappointments are God's appointments." Unknown

We all have expectations, and, to our detriment, we often come into a marriage with unreasonable expectations. Books, magazines, television, and movies have given all of us a false vision of how a couple will always experience joy and fulfillment in marriage. But, on the contrary, the truth is that not every couple will own a house with a white picket fence. But, of course, not every husband will have a well-paying job. Not every wife will have lunch with her wondrously, happy friends every day. The Prince Charming may not live up to the wife's expectations which can cause disillusionment in the marriage.

A man and woman come into a marriage from different family backgrounds, different life experiences, different personalities, and different expectations. Expectations can be high or low, reasonable, or unreasonable. Some expect too much, and others expect too little. Either way, disappointment, and pain can ensue. These unmet expectations can cause trouble in relationships.

The culture breeds greed and an entitlement mentality. Satan uses these platforms to cause frustration in our lives and relationships, especially in marriage. For example, a woman marries a man with a great job, but he loses his job. The company was restructured, and his position was eliminated. Now the couple struggles financially, and she never expected this to happen. Her security is threatened. Resentment takes hold of her emotions because her expectations are unrealized. On the other side, the man had a mother who was a great cook. He assumes that his wife will be as adept at cooking as his mother. When she does not meet his expectation, he feels let down. Both of them have looked to one another to make them happy and secure. Both have unfair expectations.

Yet, the Bible is clear that only God is our hope. In Psalm 138:8, we read, *"The Lord will fulfill his purpose for me..."* and in Matthew 6:33, we read, *"But seek first the kingdom of God and his righteousness, and all these things will be added to you."* It is unfair to assume that another person is responsible for our joy or fulfillment. Only the Creator God knows me (Psalm 139:1). He knows what I need to satisfy my deepest longings.

Some years ago, Dennis and I were going through a low spot in our marriage. In discussions later, we discovered that our unspoken and unmet expectations had driven us apart. We each had a different perspective on the same subject. After years of marriage, the differences caused genuine harm to our future as a couple. Satan used these differences to drive a wedge between us, and we were almost side-lined in the ministry and marriage. If only we had addressed our expectations, much heartache could have been prevented. God, however, does not waste hard times in our lives. Instead, he uses them to take us deeper into our faith and trust in Him. We learned to trust Him, pray, wait and watch His hand move. We also learned that we needed to talk about our expectations. Joseph's words ring true (Genesis 50:20) that Satan meant to harm us, but God used this season to cause our faith to grow and to give us a stronger marriage. Our disappointment was God's appointment to take us into new understanding about ourselves, our marriage, and His provision.

Let's pray today for clarity in regards to our expectations with one another. Do we harbor contempt from an unrealized expectation from our spouse? We can confess it to one another. God has said that He alone is God and we are to put no other god before Him. Our spouse is not our God. Our spouse is not the source of joy or any other emotion. Commit to trust the Lord with all your hearts and to not lean to your own understanding. After you pray, you may need to resolve an issue where an unmet expectation has caused a barrier in your relationship. Ask the Lord for wisdom. (James 1:5) Don't forget: *"Be kind to one another, tenderhearted, forgiving one another, as God in Christ forgave you." Ephesians 4:32*

Join us in prayer for Day 12
at www.strategicrenewal.com/21days

STORMS OF LIFE

Dennis Henderson

"In the eye of the storm, you remain in control
And in the middle of the war, You guard my soul
You alone are the anchor when my sails are torn
Your love surrounds me in the eye of the storm."

Ray Stevenson – song -Eye of the Storm

"There are no limits to God's rule. He is never helpless,
never frustrated, never at a loss. Whenever God acts,
He acts in a way that pleases Him. God is never constrained to do
a thing that He despises. He is never backed into a corner where
His only recourse is to do something He hates to do.
He does whatever He pleases." John Piper

It was a great Saturday in May 2018. Billie and I did our routine four-mile speed walk-jog. In prior years we would run. But, due to a total knee replacement for me seven months earlier, the doctor recommended that the impact of running would not be advisable. So, we changed our regiment. We topped the afternoon with a full circuit workout at Nautilus. The next day was not as glorious. It was 6:05 AM. I had just finished my quiet time and was sitting at my desk in my office at home looking at my sermon notes. A severe pain struck my right leg. To make a long story short, I was paralyzed from the waist down by a spinal stroke. Less than 1% of people who have strokes experience a spinal stroke. After weeks in a rehab hospital, I walk with a gimp in my step and deal with pain and spasticity twenty-four hours a day, managed with muscle relaxers and pain pills. I work out regularly to keep my legs from atrophy. It appears this will be my situation until I get healing in heaven.

One thing we are guaranteed in life is trouble. It began when Adam and Eve sinned. Some of our problems are self-inflicted. However, much of them are the result of the fall. The storms come in various ways: Financial, physical, relational, situational. We must deal with cars breaking down, kids getting sick, job losses, bills piling up. Most likely, you can write your list. Why bring this to your attention today? Because the storms of life can bring stress into the marriage, as you know. Let's think through what we need to focus on amid turmoil. So I draw your attention to a doctrine in the Bible we call the sovereignty of God.

I am learning that in our chaotic world, the sovereignty of God gives me assurance and peace. Sovereignty can be defined as having supreme authority, control, and power over all that has happened, is happening, and will happen in the future. Simply put, for believers, it is the biblical truth that God is in complete control of everything, and there is nothing that is done that is not done by or allowed through His will.

Over a hundred verses tell us of the varied aspects of God's sovereignty. First, we read story after story in the Scripture where we see His wisdom and authority played out in the lives of individuals, kings, and nations. "Our God is in the heavens; He does all that He pleases" (Psalm 115:3).

"You are good and do good; teach me your statutes" (Psalm 119:68). For me, this has to be the foundation to understanding

God's sovereignty. Applying the great truth of sovereignty must be the basis of trusting God when we do not understand His ways. He is good. This deals with His character. I believed that for years. Then the following phrase declares, "He does good." This is where theology and life meet. This is where truth is tested in our lives when our circumstances do not resound that He does good. It seems like He just allowed or ordered severely.

The last phrase of the verse cannot be ignored: "teach me your statutes." Learning God's statutes, His ways take more than a Bible study at times. This is the hard part of the laboratory of life. As most pastors do, I love to teach God's truth. Sometimes, I am not as excited about learning it beyond the classroom. Is God good? Does He do good? Those questions ran through my mind for many hours at night when I was in the hospital, not knowing the future.

I am learning that the sovereignty of God is more than a doctrine. It is the reality of a trusting, dependent relationship with God who is good. The goal for all believers is that God will be glorified in their lives. Thus, the reality of deeper trust, prayer life, and clarity of purpose must be a learning laboratory during this season. We are called to live in faith and dependence each day. "Thy Kingdom come, thy will be done on earth as it is in heaven" is a prayer of sovereignty. Whether you see your circumstances as good or bad today, that is not the reality God sees. His goal is to conform us to His image; thus, we must trust that He is good and does good.

I do not know your status today in marriage, your kids, or your circumstances. If you are in the storm, meditate on Psalms 119:68. Read it repeatedly. Embrace the words of Ray Stevenson's song. Look it up and listen to it. Do not let the storms cause doubt. With a focus on God's goodness and His past blessings, you can bring your requests to Him. Complain if necessary. He knows. Follow the instructions of Paul in Philippians 4:6-8. "Do not be anxious about anything, but in every situation, by prayer and petition, with thanksgiving, present your requests to God. 7 And the peace of God, which transcends all understanding, will guard your hearts and your minds in Christ Jesus. We will join as fellow storm travelers and pray that His peace will surround your hearts.

Join us in prayer for Day 13

at www.strategicrenewal.com/21days

DAY 14

FIDELITY

Dennis Henderson

Proverbs 5:15 (NLT) "Drink water from your own well—
share your love only with your wife.
¹⁷ You should reserve it for yourselves.
Never share it with strangers.
¹⁸ Let your wife be a fountain of blessing for you.
Rejoice in the wife of your youth."

Hebrews 14:4 (The Message) "Honor marriage, and guard the
sacredness of sexual intimacy between wife and husband. God draws
a firm line against casual and illicit sex."

Satan never bothered Adam until he got married. Always remember, Satan has one desire for marriage, society, and individuals: to steal, kill, and destroy. Knowing that a godly marriage is the bedrock of an orderly society for the proclamation of the gospel, Satan will always have his focus on destroying a marriage.

As we enter marriage, it's easy to think that only "other people" get divorced, that your marriage is somehow immune to heartache. So, we say, "to death do us part" when we recite our vows with all good intentions. We do not plan on infidelity or divorce. After all, how many of us would walk down the aisle if we believed our relationships would end up in divorce court?

If you take the time to google about marital affairs and unfaithfulness, you will find a wide range of statistics. To save you time, I can tell you that the findings are not encouraging as we live in a time when marriage and Biblical morality are losing their influence. The saddening part, according to Dave Carder's and Duncan Jaenicke's book, Torn Asunder: Recovering from Extramarital Affairs, Carder notes that adultery and divorce rates in the evangelical population are nearly the same as the general population in the United States. Being a Christian does not lessen our chances of having an affair. Consequently, the divorce rate of Christian marriages is about the same as non-Christians. In over fifty years of dealing with couples, I have dealt with numerous cases of infidelity. Everyone was filled with regret. No one had any measure of joy.

There is ample information that tells us that Biblical marriage is an endangered species. Where do fidelity and infidelity begin? The direction of our lives comes from our hearts, our thinking. The heart is the place of volition, emotion, decision. Proverbs 4:23 (NLT) "Guard your heart above all else, for it determines the course of your life." We could build a list of foolish things that can draw our hearts away from our spouses. A common initiator of infidelity is developing a relationship with a member of the opposite sex, which includes conversations of problems in your marriage. Billie and I teach couples that our best friends with whom we share our concerns, marriage struggles, and personal matters cannot be someone of the opposite sex as it can pull us to emotional involvement. Also, we teach them to safeguard themselves from being alone with the opposite sex, even in working situations. With the easy access on our phones to about anything we desire, it is common sense to guard what we watch or read as everything that enters our eyes enters our hearts. What dwells in our hearts can set the course of our actions.

I could write pages about practices and protection. However, this is not a marriage manual. So, let me draw your attention to the verses listed above. Because marriage intimacy is sacred according to the passage in Hebrews and many other indications in scripture, I urge you to focus on the verses given from Proverbs. To both husband and wife, I charge you to keep focused on the one you married years ago. They are still the spouse of your youth. We mature, discover each other's flaws, and have been hurt and caused hurt. We have come short of each other's expectations. However, we can find the same passion and joy we had in our youth. We must focus on the one we committed our lives to in the covenant of marriage. It was a lifelong covenant with God as our witness. It was not a prison unless our selfishness allowed it to be. It was designed to promise protection, with boundaries established by love.

There are more divorces happening today in marriages of 25 years and more than at any time in history. Billie and I are approaching our 57th year of marriage. We both would tell you that our love, intimacy, and pleasure are greater today than at any time in our marriage. We do rejoice in the wife and the husband of our youth. We tell each other every day that we are grateful for each other. The first words we say each morning are "I love you." You might ask, "Has our love and intimacy of thought, emotion, heart been this strong throughout our marriage?" The honest answer is no. We have always loved each other. However, distractions, busyness, lack of gratitude, prayer, time together with God dulled our love. I mentioned in the introduction that we did not have fervent prayer together for many years. The lack of prayer together brought distance, isolation, and truthfully a train wreck in our 28th year of marriage.

What has brought us to the best years of our marriage to rejoice in the mate of our youth? The change of my priorities from the church to marriage. Fresh and more time together. And, got it, prayer. It keeps our hearts from wondering. Praying together guards our hearts. It causes us to have the most intimate conversations and emotions in our years of marriage. I will assure you that regularly praying intensely together with scriptures-fed prayers will do more for your marriage than anything else. It will build trust, closeness, tenderness, and oneness that will not come by any other means. Fidelity comes from the heart. The heart full of Jesus, prayer, and His Word will bring forth fidelity and gladness. You will rejoice in the spouse of your youth 57 years later.

Today, I consider it a great privilege and joy to pray with you for God to guard your heart and bring about the most significant years of romance and commitment until death do you part.

Join us in prayer for Day 14
at www.strategicrenewal.com/21days

PRAYING FOR OUR LITTLE ONES

Billie Henderson

"Sons are a heritage from the Lord, children a reward from him.
Like arrows in the hands of a warrior are sons born in one's youth.
Blessed is the man whose quiver is full of them."
Psalm 127:3-5a

We live in a culture that either neglects children or, the very opposite, worships them. Either extreme is wrong. According to the Scriptures, our children are rewards from the Almighty God. C.S. Lewis wrote: "Children are not a distraction from more important work. They are the most important work." Once we become parents, we must seriously consider the weightiness of the responsibility of training and caring for a living soul, though small, created in the likeness of God. We are charged with their physical, mental, emotional, and spiritual welfare. Now, that is a grave task! We need help!

I felt the joy as any young married woman when they were assured that they were about to become a mother. I couldn't get home fast enough to tell my husband, call our parents, and share the good news with my friends. I knew my life would change, but it would be a good change. There would be bottles, diapers, sleepless nights, little fingerprints smudged everywhere, scattered toys around the living room, but it would be worth it. That was just manual labor anyway. The reality hit me when I brought my precious treasure home from the hospital and the seriousness of being responsible for my baby girl was overwhelming. I had worked during my high school years and rarely ever babysat. So what did I know about taking care of a baby? My husband knew more about such things than I did because he had a baby brother during his middle school years. He had helped in the care of his baby brother. I was a novice! I was a mother in training! My baby daughter deserved better. Help! I'm a mother!

I discovered that the mundane activities of motherhood were manageable, but the challenges came when I started training my little one to be a disciplined human being. The greater goal was to make Jesus a reality and teach biblical truths to a child day by day. I was not going to be good enough. It was true, but God was! I read a quote by Ruth Bell Graham. "As a mother, my job is to take care of the possible and trust God with the impossible." Years later, I came across what Paul David Tripp wrote: "So your hope as a parent is not found in your power, your wisdom, your character, your experience, or your success, but in this one thing alone: the presence of your Lord. The Creator, Savior, Almighty, Sovereign King is with you. Let your heart rest. You are not in this parenting drama alone. Your potential is greater than the size of your weaknesses because the One who is without weakness is with you, and he does his best work through those who admit that they are weak but in weakness still heed his call."

Prayer became a significant part of the daily routine. When the baby slept, the Lord and I became more intimate. There was much to pray about because I was a new Christian. I was still growing in my faith and, I needed to concentrate on sharing my faith with this child as I lived it out before her. Should we not claim and pray back in confidence Isaiah 54:13: "All your children shall be taught by the Lord, and great shall be the peace of your children."? God hears our prayers as new parents. He wants to teach and lead us into the discipleship of our children.

There is also a caution to be approached. The world does not revolve around my baby or toddler. They are not gods. God is God, and He wants us to have no other gods before us. In truth, our children belong to the Lord. He will take care of them. Our every attention shouldn't be on them. Our attention is to desire God, live in His truth, and model the life of faith before our children. There are times when we as couples need to be together alone without our babies. The marriage relationship is the first relationship that should take priority. There are opportunities God gives us to meet the needs of others and which will mess up our child's nap schedule for a time. Our commitment to the body of believers at our church is important too. At times, our charity and generosity might mean our child doesn't get the latest toy and wear the best clothes. Our lifestyle is a testimony of the spiritual maturity our little ones need to see as they grow into childhood and beyond. Modeling the life of Christ involves these sorts of things that our little ones need to see. This is a balancing act, so as couples, we need to ask God to show us His will in this matter as well. Our little ones are our first disciples. They are God's disciples, so we need to be cognoscente of that. He is their God. We are not! Although they are young, they need to learn this at the outset, and so do we as parents.

So today, as you pray for young children, your baby or toddler, let us acknowledge to the Lord that there is a human deficit in parenting. As parents, grandparents, teachers, friends, to young ones, we need God's help. Pray for yourself and others to desire a genuine intimate life with Christ and model it before the little children. Pray for the toddler to have an open heart to God as they grow and to love others, for this is the second greatest commandment that Jesus gave His disciples. Ask the Lord to replace your deficiencies with His provision and wisdom. It takes more than a village to reach a child.

It takes the village and God! Pray always, at all times, for the next generation in your life.

"From the lips of children and infants you have ordained praise...".
Psalm 8:2

"When Jesus saw this, he was indignant. He said to them,
"Let the little children come to me, and do not hinder them, for the
kingdom of God belongs to such as these." Mark 10:14

These toddlers grow into childhood, and the parent is aware of the challenges. Teaching is thrust into a higher gear and pace.

"Don't let anyone look down on you because you are young,
but set an example for the believers in speech, in life, in love,
in faith and purity." I Timothy 4:12

"Your greatest contribution to the Kingdom of God may not be
something you do, but someone you raise." —Andy Stanley

Parenting skills are a continuing educational pursuit. Each child is a case study by himself. Even though I have twin daughters, they have different personalities that respond to the same situation differently. The challenge is knowing how to train and instruct children in their particular way of learning. God must hear from us daily about each child. He is their Creator, and His desire is that they would reach their full potential, contribute to His Kingdom's growth, and bring Him glory. We may not be perfect parents, but we can be praying parents.

Jesus grew in wisdom and stature and favor with God and man. That sort of sets our course. We have to instill worldly common sense and godly wisdom. We have to teach them relational skills, godly principles for righteous living before God and man, how to submit to the authorities in their lives, and how to care for the welfare of others. Their behaviors and their words are important. How can we accomplish all of this without seeking God? We can't! Our attention to prayer will reap a return. Pray, pray, pray! Be determined and disciplined.

So today, as you pray for young children, your baby or toddler, let us acknowledge to the Lord that there is a human deficit in parenting. As parents, grandparents, teachers, friends, to young ones, we need God's help. Pray for yourself and others to desire a genuine intimate life with Christ and to model it before the children. Pray for each child to have an open heart to God as they grow and to love others, for this is the second greatest commandment that Jesus gave His disciples. Pray that the older children will listen to and obey the instruction. Pray that they would grow in favor with God and man. Ask the Lord to replace your deficiencies with His provision and wisdom.

Join us in prayer for Day 15
at www.strategicrenewal.com/21days

Day 16

PRAYING FOR
OUR TEENAGERS

Billie Henderson

"Dscipline your son, and he will give you rest; he will give delight to your heart." Proverbs 29:17

"Do not be conformed to this world, but be transformed by the renewal of your mind, that by testing you may discern what is the will of God, what is good and acceptable and perfect." Romans 12:2

Parenting a teen in today's culture is hard. The culture no longer has any boundaries. What was once good is now accepted as wrong, and what is wrong is taken as good. There are no common standards to keep society in check. Teens are bombarded by social media on all fronts, and parents have to have a counter-strategy to combat the amoral lifestyles their teens are confronting daily. The biblical view regarding the subject of sex is mocked. The LGBTQ community promotes their lifestyle as natural. Drugs are readily available. Bullying and peer pressure can cause many poor decisions by our teens as they long to fit in with their peers. Video games can consume their time and distort what reality is. While all of this surrounds them, they are at a stage in their lives where they are beginning to draw away from parents and growing into independence, as is the normal progression into adulthood.

One of the dilemmas of parenting is dealing with these challenges in our teens' lives. As parents, prayer is an excellent resource for wisdom and unity in approaching these problematic issues. Over the years, Dennis and I have had to call out to God for patience, discernment, and His power to deal with the immediate problem we were facing with our children. As God impressed the way forward, we determined the needed discipline. Discipline is not a negative word but a positive word. Discipline is training. The proverb says that parents are to train their kids and then the result will be good for both parent and child. Teaching our teens biblical truth is vital for their victory over the decadent culture where they live. They need to learn that their identity is in Christ not in conforming to the ways of their friends and the culture. Parents need to look for opportunities to teach biblical truth as daily life happens: traveling in the car, doing chores together, conversation at the dinner table, truthfully answering questions as they arise. The Word of God needs to take deep root in their minds.

> *4"Hear, O Israel: The Lord our God, the Lord is one.[a]*
> *5You shall love the Lord your God with all your heart and with*
> *all your soul and with all your might. 6And these words*
> *that I command you today shall be on your heart.*
> *7You shall teach them diligently to your children, and shall talk*
> *of them when you sit in your house, and when you walk by*
> *the way, and when you lie down, and when you rise.*
> *8You shall bind them as a sign on your hand, and they shall be as*
> *frontlets between your eyes. 9You shall write them on the doorposts*
> *of your house and on your gates." Deuteronomy 6:4-9*

Modeling how the Scripture instructs our behavior, thinking, and decision-making needs to be shared with transparency and honesty. What we want for our teens must be what we practice. This is teaching: the discipline that comes from our own lives. Ask the Lord to give you a determined intention to discipline your own life first and to reveal when the times of opportunities are present to share with your teens. Pray that God would cause your teen(s) to *"Take firm hold of instruction, do not let go; keep her, for she is your life." Proverbs 4:13.*

Dennis and I have four children. The middle two are twin girls who, since they were 14 years old, have been very outspoken. I have appreciated that about them, but I have also been disappointed and fearful at what some conversations revealed. We mostly knew what they were thinking, which was in itself a challenge. Could they not be more diplomatic? One night we four discussed the Christian lifestyle. To our dismay, we heard this statement: "Dad and Mom, you chose this life of ministry for yourselves, but we want to see what else is out there." They thought that some of our rules were only necessary because Dennis was a pastor. We explained that their assumption was wrong. Our family code would be the same whether we were in full-time ministry or not. Did they "hear" what we said? No, I think they dismissed our perspective completely. The conversation eventually concluded, and we left their bedroom quite disillusioned. What direction would they choose?

Only God can change hearts. Did we go to fierce battle on our knees? You bet. All through their high school years, we faced challenges. They were never outright disobedient, but their hearts were not bent toward God whole-heartedly. Pray, pray, we did! So, they went off to college, and we prayed. Time passed, and we cried out to God for the girls. They are mothers now and there is evidence that they fully believe God's Word. They go to church and have many of the same rules for their children as we had for them. God in His timing has answered our prayers.

Our youngest child is a boy. Unlike his sisters, he was an easily led child. He had a heart for God and had, as a young kid, a desire to go into full-time ministry. During high school, he went to church, attended the youth group, and obeyed us, but around his junior year, he quit talking about going into ministry. He decided that teaching high school English and coaching high school soccer up in a mountain community to be a lay youth pastor would fit him better. He had seen ministry up close and wasn't sure that was what he wanted to deal with the rest of his life. As a mom, that was a good call. It was a good choice. Dennis and I prayed that he would continue to grow spiritually no matter what profession he chose. The goal wasn't to have a son in the ministry.

In his senior year's fourth game of soccer, he tore his ACL. Surgery was imminent. The disappointment was that he could not accept scholarship offers to play college soccer. On the way to the hospital, his despair was poignant. "I don't get it. I have not gone to parties. I have treated girls rightly. I have been involved at church, and THIS is what God lets happen to me!" My mother's heart sensed his grief and dismay. My husband was quiet and just drove. The only thing I could say was, "Denny, the Bible says, *"'For I know plans I have for you,' declares the Lord, 'plans to prosper you and not to harm you, plans to give you a hope and a future.'" (Jeremiah 29:11)* I honestly could not think of anything else to say. We rode in silence for the next 20 minutes. We prayed for Denny's recovery and for God's will to be revealed to him (yes, and to us) over the next few months. The youth group went to winter camp in January, and Denny could join them as his knee was well on its way to healing. For us at home, life just went on. God was at work though. When Denny returned, he was a happy guy. He told Dennis and me that he had given his life to full-time ministry. He graduated high school and went to a local junior college for a year while his knee healed. God shows up for His glory! Denny received a scholarship to play soccer at a college in southern California. He has married a wonderful woman. They have three children, and he is happily pastoring a church in Texas. Believing and speaking God's Word to our children is pivotal as we do life together. It is intentionally done. It must be a part of who we are.

As you pray today, ask God to give you wisdom and a determined pursuit to teach your children to live well under God's authority. Pray for your teen to have strong faith to help them live above their circumstances and have the confidence that all things will work together for their good. The Bible says, *"And we know that for those who love God all things work together for good, for those who are called according to his purpose." Romans 8:28*

Join us in prayer for Day 16
at www.strategicrenewal.com/21days

PRAYING FOR
OUR ADULT CHILDREN

Billie Henderson

*"And this is the confidence that we have toward him,
that if we ask anything according to his will, he hears us. And if we
know that he hears us in whatever we ask, we know that we have the
request that we have asked of him." I John 5:14-15*

*"Now to him who is able to do far more abundantly than all that we
ask or think, according to the power at work within us. To him be glory
in the church and in Christ Jesus throughout all generations, forever
and ever. Amen." Ephesians 3:20-21*

*"You can't go back and change the beginning, but you can start where
you are and change the ending." C. S. Lewis*

Life is a comedy. When our children leave our homes, we think our job is now finished. They are now on their own even though they still call us "dad" and "mom." Our concern for their well-being does not change. What is changing, we discover quickly, is that we no longer have control over them. They will do what they want and when they want to do it. We will not know all of the details of their lives, thoughts, decisions, new relationships, and actions. Our time with them is now limited. This is a new reality for us. The connection is changed, and so now we release them. What can we do? They surely need our help! Indeed, life is a comedy.

The culture is worse than when we left our parents' homes, for the influences surrounding our adult children are exponentially more decadent. The enemy of every soul is on the warpath to destroy, kill and steal. Our influence is no longer as loud as the clamor of the world where they are spending their time, so we can and must fervently pray for them. Our prayers can keep them from the enemy's schemes to destroy their lives. Our prayers have the power to keep them on the right path and help them live in God's will for their individual lives. We can still impact their relationship with God, mental and emotional health, decisions, marriages, parenting, and so much more. No one knows our children as we do, and no one loves them as we do. Of course, that is not a valid statement! The Creator God, who is love, knows them better and loves them greater than our earthy love ever can. He not only hears our earnest prayers, but He will do exceedingly more than we expect, for His love produces the greatest of results. Our heart's cries for our adult children will be attended to by the King of Glory, the Great I AM!

"Arise, cry out in the night, at the beginning of the night watches! Pour out your heart like water before the presence of the Lord! Lift your hands to him for the lives of your children..." Lamentations 2:17

As parents, probably each one of us carries some guilt for not always doing everything well. We made mistakes. Some of us carry the heavyweight of responsibility, and we may even blame ourselves for our adult child's mistakes, but may I encourage you. First of all, I am only aware of one perfect father, the Heavenly Father. We are imperfect human beings. Christ died for our guilt and shame, so we can confess our mistakes and receive complete forgiveness from the Father. If needed, we can ask our adult children for forgiveness too. Then, we move forward as forgiven parents. C. S. Lewis was correct. "You can't go back and change the beginning, but you can start where you are and change the ending." Today, we have to do our best for our grown kids and bless them with our prayers. God hears our prayers, and He works. When we are weak, we can have full confidence that God can fill in the gaps. He knows what our kids need and how to open their hearts for change so, we pray, pray, and keep on praying.

"Continue steadfastly in prayer, being watchful in it with thanksgiving." Colossians 4:2

"If you then who are evil, know how to give good gifts to your children, how much more will your Father who is in heaven give good things to those who ask him!" Matthew 7:11

Having prayed for our children through the years, I have seen so many answers to our prayers. One prayer has always been that our children would one day have Christian spouses. I wonder how many times we said, "Every date is a potential mate." After our twins graduated high school, we moved the family to California. The twins each had a guy they perceived to be in their future. They were so young, but I was only 18 when I married Dennis, so there was not much that I could say. So, we prayed for these young men and for God's will to play out in both girls' relationships. About a year had passed, and these relationships were still progressing, much to my surprise. One of the young men had joined the Marines. He was going to join the war in Iraq. He came for a visit and asked my husband for permission to ask our daughter to marry him. Since we had prayed, we trusted in God to work out His will in our daughter's life. We decided to support their decision for marriage and continued our praying. We could see some stumbling blocks down the road for both of them, and these issues need some discussion.My daughter listened. Her fiance' left for the Middle East. She began planning their wedding. She bought her dress, had her announcements picked out and ordered, had her wedding court ready to go, and her flowers and decorations prepared for order as well. The war ended quickly, and her fiance returned to the states. So, he came for a visit and left much of his stuff with us. The Marines sent him to Dallas to do recruiting. To our dismay, she never heard from him again. As parents, your empathy is bruising. We watched her disappointment and struggle to carry on. She continued her junior college studies, received her AA, and transferred to a university to get her BA. While she was there, she managed the five-star restaurant at the airport. She met the nicest and hardest working young man and fell in love. After finishing their degrees, they married. They are parents of two boys and are both principals in two different schools. They are both Christians and involved in their local church. God blessed our family. He heard our prayers, and He orchestrated events so our daughter could have a better life. Prayer was crucial in restoring our daughter's hopes and dreams and giving her a prosperous future. All Dennis and I did was pray, pray, and pray some more.

We have seen God answer so many prayers for our adult children. When they make major decisions, they always share their concerns and ask us to pray for them. Our input is still important to them and they desire our prayers regarding their decisions as they lead their families and serve others.

Like any family we have struggles and hard times. Our son, the pastor, was diagnosed with clinical depression at the same time that he and his wife were told that their third child would have down syndrome. The months moved slowly and it was dismal on all fronts. We prayed. We needed God to restore mental health to our son and to protect his wife and family during this tough season. There was nothing easy during these years. I can proudly say God is so powerful. Our son is pastoring again. He is not on medication. Our grandson has had few health issues and has surpassed the doctor's original assessment of his abilities. I give my daughter-in-law credit for some of that. She is remarkable. Little River is a blessing to our family. God has done immeasurably more than we have expected. Every tearful prayer He has heard and then responded. His glory is on display for all to see. Our faith has matured. Prayer made the difference.

During this horrific season, I also had a group of friends praying with me. One tearful morning, they gathered around me. They laid their hands on me and they prayed in faith with great agony for my son, his family, and Dennis and me. They approached God's throne with praise, passion and boldness. Those prayers still reverberate in my mind and are in that golden bowl before the throne of God echoing through eternity. God keeps His Word to us. He responds to the prayers of His people.

"When you pass through the waters, I will be with you; and through the rivers, they shall not overwhelm you; when you walk through fire you shall not be burned, and the flame shall not consume you." Isaiah 43:2

"Truly, I say to you, whatever you bind on earth shall be bound in heaven, and whatever you loose on earth shall be loosed in heaven. Again I say to you, if two of you agree on earth about anything they ask, it will be done for them by my Father in heaven." Mathew 18:18-19

As you go to prayer today, go boldly. Agree together as you pray for your adult children. (If you don't have adult children yet, pray for your little ones' futures as regards to their adult decisions and their hearts to desire God.) Pray that they will have open hearts to God and desire intimacy with Him, longing to read His Word and do life according to His ways. Ask the Lord to protect them from the evil influences in the culture and sexual immorality. If they seem far from God, ask God to cause them to feel the need for His help. Pray that they see their identity in Christ and know God's purpose for their lives. Pray over their marriages and their parenting. If they are going through rough times, ask God to strengthen them and to provide what they need. They may need restoration and wholeness. Ask God to restore them and give them abundant living. Ask the Holy Spirit to guide your prayer for He knows your adult children's greatest needs today. Your influence is mighty. Your love can cover a multitude of sins through your heart cries to God for your kids. *"And the peace of God, which surpasses all understanding, will guard your hearts and your minds in Christ Jesus." Philippians 4:7*

Join us in prayer for Day 17
at www.strategicrenewal.com/21days

PRODIGALS

Dennis Henderson

Luke 15:11 "And he said, "There was a man who had two sons.
¹²And the younger of them said to his father,
'Father, give me the share of property that is coming to me.'
And he divided his property between them. ¹³Not many days
later, the younger son gathered all he had and took his journey into a
far country, and there wasted his substance with reckless living."

"Every parent is at some time the father of the unreturned prodigal,
with nothing to do but keep the house open." John Ciardi

The prodigal: "We all know one, have been one, or waiting on one to
come home." Unknown

When parents pray over the little ones they hold in their arms, they never expect them to break their hearts. All they sense is a response of love, dependence, and bonding. In those early days, they could not imagine that the parable Jesus told over 2,000 years ago would be the story of their child. The story Jesus tells in Luke 15 is one of the most known parables of the gospels. The term prodigal is used in church and secular settings. It is a description of rebellion, waste, and futility.

I do not have to give a complete account of the story. We know the talking points. There was a young son who asked for his inheritance early. He leaves against the wishes of his father and the customs of the day. In a far land, he wastes his money on foolish living. There were the parties, the prostitutes, and the spending of funds to be accepted by the wrong crowd. So, he ends up broke, working a despised job in the pigpen.

How do parents respond when a child travels this path? There is devastation, heartache, shame, and embarrassment. They start to feel like they have failed and that their experience is rare. I remind parents that the very first family with Adam and Eve had a prodigal. Priests and prophets of the Old Testament like Eli and Samuel had prodigals. The children of God, the Israelites, lived in an ongoing prodigal status. Jesus' disciples went the wrong path when he needed their support the most. Peter became known as one who denied him. Some of the most renowned leaders you may know had prodigal sons, Luis Palau, Billy Graham, John Piper, John Ortberg. I do not point these out with a critical eye as I, too, have had a prodigal. So, if you are a parent with a prodigal today, know you are not alone. There have been thousands before and will be thousands after you.

I offer you a few points of guidance and prayer during the prodigal season you might be experiencing.

First, pray for insight into your feelings about your rebellious child. Russell Moore gives some good advice, "This pain shouldn't be confused, though, with our carnal desire to display to the world around us what "blessed" and "successful" families we have. In many cases, the real tragedy in a family with rebellious children isn't that their parents hurt for them, but that their parents are embarrassed by them. If "good" children were the result of mere technique, then we could boast of our own righteousness through the lives of our children. They're not." Know your children's choices do not always reflect your parenting.

Second, pray that you will release your children to God. We have a daughter who was prodigal for over twenty-five years. One of the issues I had to deal with was that of rescue. I academically knew all about enabling. I would advise parents to stop enabling their children. Yet emotionally, I could not practice my own advice until a good friend who was a counselor said to me, "Your daughter's problem is your addiction." She went on to explain my addiction was rescuing her. Vance Havner, known for his straightforwardness and humor, reflected on the story. "If they had had a social gospel in the days of the prodigal son, somebody would have given him a bed and sandwiches, and he would never have come home." Releasing my daughter into God's hands for his work in her life was difficult.

Pray for whatever it takes to bring them home. I remind you of one part of the story that we sometimes overlook was the famine. It took a famine for the son to come to his senses. The famine brought about despair and hunger, which were the best part for him in a far country. So, pray that God will do whatever is necessary to bring your child back to the Father. Remember that God works all things together for our good. (Romans 8:28). This might include bad for the ultimate good.

Pray for your heart and attitude to reflect God's character with patience, kindness, and love. It is easy to allow a hard heart to form after years of pain. In your times of frustrations and anger, call out to God to give you His steadfast love. Galatians 6:9 tells us not to grow weary in well-doing. Remember, Romans 2:4 tells us that the kindness of God brings us to repentance.

Pray for your marriage. The priority of human relationships and family is the relationship of husband and wife. Pray that God will help you keep that in perspective and remind you to nourish it amid the confusion and frustration of your prodigal. I have dealt with many couples whose children's sinful lifestyles impacted their marriage. This is a time to draw close, spend time together without the topic of your prodigal absorbing you. Find enjoyment together that balances your sorrow.

Pray with hope remembering the mighty hand of God. Romans 15:13 "May the God of hope fill you with all joy and peace in believing, so that by the power of the Holy Spirit you may abound in hope." Don't forget the many passages of God's ability to change hearts as he has changed history on many occasions.

Last, pray the scriptures. Go through the Psalms and many other places that give you God's perspective and depend on the passages. Job 42:2; Isaiah 59:1; Psalm 107:14,15. Proverbs 16:9. There are many, many more. Praying His word will always soften our words.

Today, with a heart of empathy, I will join you in praying for your child. I encourage you that God can bring the prodigal home. After twenty-five years of horrible decisions, shattered relationships, drugs, and bipolar battles, God can bring a child home. We have been there, and praying together got us through.

Join us in prayer for Day 18
at www.strategicrenewal.com/21days

Day 19

CULTURE

Dennis Henderson

Daniel continued through a culture unlike his own; one that lost its way. Today, you and I are living in a culture that's losing its way. It's good to know that just as in Daniel's day, God is looking for men and women of integrity to help confront in love a culture that's losing its way and to point it back to him. O. S. Hawkins

"The culture is your friend in the same way that a brown bear is your buddy. L. Page Patterson

John 17:15 "I do not ask that you take them out of the world, but that you keep them from the evil one. ¹⁶They are not of the world, just as I am not of the world. ¹⁷Sanctify in the truth; your word is truth. ¹⁸As you sent me into the world, so I have sent them into the world."

Romans 12:2 "Do not be conformed to this world, but be transformed by the renewal of your mind, that by testing you may discern what is the will of God, what is good and acceptable and perfect."

1 John 2:15 "Do not love the world or the things in the world. Anyone loves the world, the love of the Father is not in him. ¹⁶For all that is in the world—the desires of the flesh and the desires of the eyes and pride of life is not from the Father but is from the world. ¹⁷And the world is passing away along with its desires, but whoever does the will of God abides forever.'

Over fifty years ago, we did not talk much about culture when I graduated college and entered graduate studies. Instead, the topic was worldliness as my strong Baptist background focused on dancing, drinking, smoking, and Hollywood movies. Today, my concern is culture. Culture includes language, habits, ideas, customs, values, social structures, and practices. It can influence our way of life.

We hear a great deal about cancel culture as I write. I am not writing to discuss the issues. However, I do believe when you dig past the title of these stated "cultures," you find many anti-biblical teachings on family, sexuality, and gender elimination. I mention this brings attention to how quickly some in our society are imposing questionable practices.

I scratch the surface of culture to alert us to how it can impact our marriage and family. I believe we can agree that we have come to the tipping point of a post-Christian society. Satan is unleashing every influence he can on what is going around us to cause us to choose other gods. The passage from 1 John 2 tells us what our culture melts down to pleasure, possession, and positions. If we are not alert to the devil's arsenal, we can be taken down. Be attentive to what is being brought into your homes. Remember, the first sin was built on a lie. Paul's explanation of sin in Romans 1 is that mankind had exchanged the truth for a lie. The Bible is true. Keep that central in your value system, conversations, and choices in your home.

In John 17, Jesus says he sent us into the world. His goal was not isolation but penetration. Yet, while being sent into the world as His ambassadors, we can find ourselves subtly chasing the same things the culture does. However, we can stand firm like Daniel in Babylon, Joseph in Egypt, Paul and the apostles in a pagan society. Our mission is to love the world as people and not as a system while giving forth the truth

The popularity of social media and cells phones is overwhelming. Facebook, Snapchat, Instagram, Twitter, Tik Tok, Texting, and Internet are in our hands hours a day. Much of the time, we use these tools in an unproductive manner. There are multiple studies of the harm cell phones can cause to a child's self-image, immoral exposure, and psychological damage. It always saddens me when I am in a restaurant and see a family dining with phones in their hands, and no conversation occurs. I always want to walk over and say, "Get your heads out of your apps." When we have family dinners at our house with our adult children and grandchildren, we place a basket at the door when they walk in to deposit their cell phones. I firmly tell parents to limit cell phone use for themselves and their children. So put on filters that alert you and your mate when the phone goes to the wrong locations of each other or your children. Guard the amount of time and exposure your children have.

The wisdom and logic of the world come at us every day. It is difficult to find a television program or movie that promotes traditional family values or any facsimile of Christian values. Paul in Colossians and James in his letter clarify this to us.

Colossians 2:8 (NIV) "See to it that no one takes you captive through hollow and deceptive philosophy, which depends on human tradition and the elemental spiritual forces of this world rather than on Christ."

James 3:17 "But the wisdom from above is first pure, then peaceable, gentle, open to reason, full of mercy and good fruits, impartial and sincere. [18]And a harvest of righteousness sown in peace by those who make peace.

As you daily pray together as a couple, saturate your prayers with the Word of God. Pray scriptures of truth back to God to guard your heart and mind so that you can be prepared to identify vain philosophies and empty lies that swirl around us. Pray for your children and with your children to know the truth, which can set us free.

We join you today in praying that we may penetrate it with love and the truth in our culture. We will pray you will not bend or bow to a culture moving away quickly from God.

Join us in prayer for Day 19
at www.strategicrenewal.com/21days

THE CHURCH

Dennis Henderson

Ephesians 5:25 "Husbands, love your wives, as Christ loved the church and gave himself up for her."

Ephesians 3:20 "Now to him who is able to do far more abundantly than all that we ask or think, according to the power at work within us, [21]to him be glory in the church and in Christ Jesus throughout all generations, forever and ever. Amen.

I was taken by a neighbor lady to her Catholic church when I was six years old. It was my first venture inside a church. It was not a good experience for me, my neighbor, or the Nunn who swatted my hand as I walked out for stealing the cup of holy water on the wall. I saw everyone dipping their fingers into it and making some motions with their hands. I thought it must be important, so I decided to take it home. I never returned to church until I reached middle school. I grew up in a non-church, non-God family until then. A young Baptist preacher's wife was drawn to my mother, who had been married five times before I had completed seventh grade. After many conversations and expressions of love, we finally went to church. Shortly after hearing the Gospel at church, my mother trusted Christ, which radically changed her life. Later, my original father was saved at the church, I trusted Christ, and we had a new family because of God using the church to invade our lives. It was through the church that Christ rescued our family. Consequently, I will always hold the church dear to my heart.

I charge every couple I marry in their wedding ceremony that three commitments will hold their marriage together. First is their daily commitment to God. Second is their daily commitment to each other. Third is their commitment to the church, the body of Christ. When the church is functioning correctly, it will be a great source of strength, encouragement, and protection for their marriage. Therefore, I turn our attention to the church for today's prayer focus.

Being employed by the church for fifty-six years now, I know and have experienced the flaws in the church. Truthfully, I have contributed to some of the shortcomings. The church is a paradox with the sweetest people I know and the meanest people. We have experienced betrayal, unjust criticism, deep hurt, and undeserved praise and recognition. I know every element of church life. I have pastored small and large churches, simple and complex.

We all know the church is not perfect. Raising four children in a pastor's home is not easy. Unfortunately, they get to experience some of the dark sides of the church. Billie and I tried not to bring the wrong part of the church home. We did not want to amplify what they already sensed. Yet, many times our family discussions crossed into the church's dirt. Yes, we dealt with their issues when asked, but the church was God's love, His bride, so we presented the church in the best posture we could. We wanted our children to love the church. Even with its shortcomings, it would be the one place that the gates of hell would not prevail.

We continue to want the church to be a place of refuge and help for our children and grandchildren after we are long gone. We want our commitment to God's church to be part of the legacy we leave in them. We want them to serve in the church and help get the Gospel out to every man, woman, and child in their community.

Place the church as a priority in your home. Display faithfulness to your local church. "Church attendance is as vital to a disciple as a transfusion of rich, healthy blood to a sick man."- Dwight L. Moody

Serve in your church. Model to your children the importance of being joined to other believers. Be part of the solution to the shortcomings in your church rather than the critics. Speak positive words to children about the church.

The church is God's plan for the world to experience God's glory, truth, love, and power. These are promises to the church. Thus, we invite you to pray today for your church. Today, we want to pray with you about your place of service. We want to pray that you are engaged and part of the life-giving people in your congregation. We encourage you to pray for unity in your church so that it will be a powerful force in your community. Pray for your pastors and your church leaders. They carry a load that many church members never know. Spend time today thanking God for your church. Pray that your children will love the church and not forsake it when they leave your home.

Join us in prayer for Day 20
at www.strategicrenewal.com/21days

LEGACY

Dennis Henderson

Psalm 78:3 "things that we have heard and known,
that our fathers have told us.
⁴We will not hide them from their children,
But tell to the coming generation
the glorious deeds of the Lord, and his might,
and the wonders that he has done."

"Our days on earth are limited, but our work for Christ is endless."
Dennis Henderson

"The great use of life is to spend it for something that will outlast it."
William James

"I glorified you on earth, having accomplished the work
that you gave me to do." Jesus

"The life of a Christian is wondrously ruled in this world,
by the consideration and meditation of the life of another world."
Richard Sibbes

On the wall in front of my desk at my office at church, I have a picture of a highway sign that says, "Finish Line Just Ahead." At 75 years old, the thought of the finish line is on my mind often. It is not threatening but one of motivation, joy, and hope as the world I live in seems more chaotic each day. I have always had the finish line in mind. But at this stage, it is like the 2-minute drill in football. The game can be decided in those last moments. No matter how tired or painful the body is, the players play their best game at this point. It is that time that the game can go either way. So, the players dig deep and press on. I awaken every day now with that thought in mind. The idea of setting the game out at this point, watching from the sideline, has no appeal. Retirement has no attraction. I will close this last day of our time together with some thoughts on your legacy.

First, have a clear understanding of legacy. I do not know where I first heard this statement or to whom to give credit, but it has never left my mind: "An inheritance is what you leave for others. A legacy is what you leave in others." Leaving an inheritance for a family is good. College money for grandkids, houses, portfolios left for the family is honorable but temporary. Leaving a life lived for God's kingdom is superior. Depositing the story of the Gospel and God's glorious deeds to your family should be our highest goal. Plan your fourth quarter with days of telling your family of the goodness and faithfulness of God over your years.

Second, I shared the finish line thought with you as I believe it has much to do with our legacies. Running to the finish leaves a memory to our children, grandchildren, friends of what is truly important. I have been saying this for some time now, "This is not home. We are here on a temporary visa." We are not home. Rest will be on the other side. Let your family see the prize of heaven lived out in your final years.

Third, store up treasures in heaven. Everything we see in this world will pass away except people. Billie and I have tried not to plant our roots deep on earth. We have intentionally, over the years, tried not to collect a lot of junk. I do not think we have made it to the new fad of being minimalists, but I do know we keep life reasonably simple. The more we collect, the more we must maintain, which involves time and money. Since both of those items are limited for us, we want to steward them for what's most productive for God's kingdom. We strongly believe we will stand before our Savior someday and give an account of how we spent our lives. Make your treasure chest people and the investments made in a kingdom that will last forever.

Fourth, this is going to sound a little strange. Write your end-of-life letter NOW. Most likely, you will not be capable of doing it in your final days. You can write one letter to all or individual notes to family members and selected friends. This letter would be what you want them to know and remember. Then, of course, you will want to share your love and gratitude. However, you should write the spiritual truths you want them to hang on to the rest of their lives. This is not morbid. It is joyous. It is sharing the joys of serving Jesus and your goals to finish well. As they think of the future, I also tell people to imagine their first moment in heaven. What do you want to hear? Whom do you want to see? I want to hear, "Well done, good and faithful servant." I want to see people with whom I had the privilege of sharing the Gospel. Most of all, I want to see the one who loves more than I could ever imagine, my Savior.

I hope that I could somehow stand in the shadow of the Apostle Paul and hope I can whisper, *"I have fought the good fight, I have finished the race, I have kept the faith. "(1 Timothy 4:7)*

Let's pray today for us to keep an eternal perspective, to seek a legacy more than an inheritance for the future. Billie and I most likely will not meet most of you this side of home or even know your name. However, our prayers will be on all those who might pick up these pages that we all will cherish our marriages, seek God's face daily together and finish well."

"But I do not account my life of any value nor as precious to myself, if only I may finish my course and the ministry I received from the Lord Jesus, to testify to the gospel of the grace of God." (Acts 20:24)

Join us in prayer for Day 21
at www.strategicrenewal.com/21days

Our Marriage Creed

We proclaim and commit that our individual and joint relationship with our God is our number one priority and seek to love Him with all our heart, with all our soul, and our mind. *Matthew 22:37, 38.*

We proclaim and commit that our love, service, care, and adoration for each other is our number two priority and will supersede all other human relationships. *Genesis 2:24; Matthew 19:5, Mark 10:8; Ephesians 5:31*

We proclaim and commit that we will always speak positively to and about each other and never belittle one another at any time in private or publicly. *Proverbs 15:23; Proverbs 15:4; Ephesians 5:29*

We proclaim and commit that forgiveness will be automatic as Christ forgave us. *Ephesians 5:32*

We proclaim and commit that we will treat each other with gentleness, meekness and kindness. *Ephesians 5:33. Colossians 3:12-13*

We proclaim and commit that we will express gratitude to each other daily, because a grateful heart is a humble and loving heart. *1 Corinthians 1:4*

We proclaim and commit that we will nourish a deep love and respect for each other which will build needed significance and security. *Ephesians 5:33*

We proclaim and commit that we will be generous to God and trust Him for our provisions and care. *2 Corinthians 9:10-15*

We proclaim and commit that we pursue a deep, active life of intimacy together and will not defile our marriage. *Hebrews 13:4; Ephesians 5:3*

We proclaim and commit that our marriage will be a picture of Christ and the Church and will live and order our lives to honor Him above all else. *Ephesians 5:25-28*

Dennis and Billie